Out of Performance, Into Identity

How Love Found Me

Angela Yarborough

Praise for *Out of Performance, Into Identity*:

"This book is so encouraging! Anyone who has struggled with consequences or dealt with poor decisions will truly be encouraged by this book. Angela's story is so real and raw that you can't help but put yourself in her shoes and pray that God delivers you the same way!"

—Tara Howington, Bible Study Sisters Club

"Powerful and relevant for every female on the planet! Angela Yarborough's story holds the keys to opening each imprisoned heart."

—Laura Wasson, 100X Family

"*Out of Performance, Into Identity*" is a captivating love story of God's persistent grace and transformative mercy. It is a more than a moving testimonial narrative, it is a welcome invitation to share in His restorative healing."

—Emilea Haddox - Bible Study Sisters

For my parents.

_____

Parenting is hard. We do our best and pray that our children turn out well. You did your best, and I think you will agree that I turned out well. Thank you for giving me the foundation I needed to become the woman I have become today.
I love you.

For my oldest girls.

_____

Parenting is hard. We do our best and pray that our children turn out well. I am so grateful that God blessed me with you. Thank you for the joy you continue to bring into my life.
I love you.

Contents

Foreword

By Sandi Sadako

When I think about Angela, words like open, authentic, safe, and fiery (in a good way) come to mind. From the first moment of meeting her in person, I felt the invitation to trust and entrust my authentic self to her in friendship. So much so that one afternoon, during a break at a conference we attended, I pulled out a file folder from my tote bag and asked if she'd like to read a couple of pages of my book in progress.

I remember standing to the side of the conference venue hallway and trying to not act nervous as Angela read one of my chapters. No one passing by knew what was taking place that day as I let someone's eyes, other than my own, rest on my yet-to-be-published book. Part of me felt nervous, wondering if what I'd written was worth including in a book for public consumption. The other part knew that the reader standing before me was trustworthy and would handle my heart on a page with tender care.

In these pages that you hold in your hand or read digitally, you'll experience the same person I did. Angela's genuinely caring, encouraging, tender heart is what you'll encounter time and time again. Her life message carries hope, promise, truth, and love.

Not to say that there aren't ups and downs. Spoiler alert, there are ups and downs; some may make you downright angry. I felt angry because of the injustices experienced by a loved one. You know the feeling; something inside rises up and wants to protect or right the wrong of the situation. These were necessary to give us a glimpse into her circumstances, decisions, and consequences.

Angela holds nothing back about her story. As a reader, I appreciated her behind-the-scenes look into her thoughts, behaviors, and emotions. Her openness may help you identify your own heart's motives, empowering you with choices and solutions.

This author lives life believing she's purely loved, wholly forgiven, and wonderfully cherished. There is lightness in her step because she knows God looks out for her and wants what's best for her. She knows she belongs in the family of God, which leads to knowing her purpose. This is a love that you will understand by the time you read to the end of this book.

It'll be worth your time. Besides, what have you got to lose? The prize is a life filled with love, the kind of love that a gal's heart is longing for, and a purpose of knowing why you were put on this earth. Go ahead, take a deep breath and start reading!

Sandi Sadako
Author of *Journey Into More*

Preface

Writing a book was never an item on my bucket list. I began this book-writing journey out of obedience to God after He spoke to me in a dream one night. Initially, I dug my heels in as I reminded Him that I was not a writer and had no intentions of ever being one. He lovingly brought me to the idea as He started sending women into my life who needed to hear my story of redemption.

As I prayed for God to show me how to teach these women to fall completely in love with Him, He told me, "Just tell your story." So, this book was born. I went from performing for love, attention, and needing to be seen and heard by others, to find validation to finding my identity in who He had created me to be.

In addition to writing this book as an act of obedience to help others, it has been a healing journey for me. I wrestled with writing it; putting this many words into written form seemed like an impossible task. It brought up beliefs I had formed about myself over the years that had become an identity for me. *Only intelligent, intellectual people write books. I am average. People want to read interesting books. I have no story to tell. For a book to sell, you must be someone famous. I am not that important.*

All these beliefs had been previously addressed in my life, and I thought I had moved forward. But what I found was interesting. As you will see in my story, I have experienced phenomenal growth. There was a lot of transformation during my journey of healing, yet there was more He wanted to do. Going from *I am not smart* to *I am average* was not good enough. Telling myself that I was better at supporting others as they built their dreams and told their stories was no longer a place for me to hide. Believing that I had nothing within myself to offer, I thought it was better to remain in the background, playing small.

I had formed a solid belief that my purpose was to cheer others on and support them as *they* pursued their calling in life. Being good at this and thoroughly enjoying seeing others rise above, I never questioned my beliefs in this identity. I could have stayed there and never known any different.

Yet, those deep desires of my heart kept surfacing. This is how great our God is. He will never let you settle for less.

If you are open to growth, He will take you to the height of your potential and show you who you were created to be. It will be the most amazing gift of discovery as you yield to His love and find total freedom from your past.

This book is my love story. I went from fighting to prove who I was and performing for the love I deeply desired, to laying down my sword and allowing Him to show me a deep love – so deep, I never thought it existed. In the middle of fighting for the love I desperately wanted, His love found me. It was there all along, I just could not see it through my brokenness.

Unlike the love I was seeking elsewhere (that would never satisfy), His love didn't need to be fought for; it only required a heart of surrender. His love has drastically changed how I look at everything. I no longer fight for love and acceptance created through others' opinions, job titles, or accomplishments. I live from a heart of freedom overflowing with passion for Him.

As I have stretched myself through this writing journey, I had no clue about the potential that was lying dormant inside me. Many days, I look at myself in the mirror and question, "Who is this girl? I flippin' love her!"

I am no longer the same person I was. Jesus has totally and completely wrecked me for His good. He has helped me gather all the missing pieces of my heart that have been stolen and put them back together in the most beautiful way. It has been a process with lots of learning, growing, and healing along the way. Praise God, I have walked it out and received the gift of His unfailing, never-ending love on the other side. His love will make every fairy tale you have ever dreamed of fall short.

As I have put my love story into words over these past months, I have been praying that you would find your own love story as we journey together. I have prayed that God will meet you in the pages, and as He heals up your broken places, you will find the love that He has been waiting to give you. I know it is possible, no matter where you find yourself today, because I have seen it happen repeatedly. I also pray for your heart to be tender and your ears open to hear how much He truly cherishes a love relationship with you.

You are special.
You are seen.
You are loved beyond measure.
You were created for a great purpose; a purpose
that only you can fulfill.

This is my story of how I overcame and found my identity and purpose. I love you, friend. As we embark on this journey of helping you discover who you are created to be, I will be your biggest cheerleader.

Welcome to my love story.

1

Once Upon a Time

Before we get started on this journey of finding love, I want to highlight some things about me that will be important to know as my story unfolds. So let me introduce myself.

My name is Angela Yarborough. Growing up, I was known as "Angie." I grew up an only child in a small Southern town out in the country. My parents loved me and brought me up in church, which was the Southern thing to do. We went to church every Sunday morning and Wednesday evening. Although I received the knowledge of who Jesus was during this time, I had not yet experienced a relationship with Him. This hearing with my young ears would later lead me to hear with my heart. I will be forever grateful that I was given this foundation of being introduced to Him.

Summer was my favorite season. While my mom worked, I spent most of those days with my grandmother. She instilled in me a love for nature, which always brought joy. We would plant gardens, pick flowers, and watch the birds from the lawn chair under the expansive magnolia tree in her front yard.

Gran taught me the secrets of planting iris bulbs. There was a particular way to plant them to ensure they would grow big, bright blooms. Her gorgeous iris blooms were proof that she knew what she was doing, as people would turn their cars around to stop and admire them. She knew how to love people, too. They would often leave with a brown paper bag of iris bulbs of their own complete with the secret planting technique.

She had the greenest thumb of anyone I knew. Every summer, we would plant a vegetable garden. After the garden grew, we would pick tomatoes, corn, butter beans, okra, and my personal favorite... cucumbers. She taught me how to shell beans, can tomatoes, and shuck the corn before blanching it to put it in the freezer. Shucking the corn was my least favorite thing to do because of the giant green worms that would often be hiding under the husks. Despite those hideous creatures, being in my grandmother's presence was worth every heartbeat skipped when uncovering one. Being with my Gran was so peaceful. Life was simple, yet every day was an adventure.

Every day had an adventure to be discovered. My imagination was larger than life. Being an only child living in the country and not having many kids around to play with gave me the perfect opportunity to develop that imagination. I was skilled in the art of entertaining myself. One day I could be a famous dancer leaping and twirling on the stage of my grandmother's back porch; the next day, you might find me as a car mechanic doing serious repairs on my bicycle chain as I took it on and off the gears. The grease covering my hands afterward made me feel like I had accomplished something massive.

I also had a great eye for attention to detail. Puzzles were one of my favorite things to do. The more pieces they contained, the better. I remember one puzzle featuring Mickey Mouse on a roller coaster with all his friends. Something stirred in me every time a piece of the puzzle would fit right into its place as the picture slowly came to life. It gave me immense pleasure to be the hands that brought seemingly insignificant parts of something together to create the big picture. Although I had put this puzzle together more times than I could count, when the last piece fit into place, it was like I was seeing its completion for the first time. A sense of accomplishment flowed through my veins as I ran my hands over the completed work. The last time I put the puzzle together, however, it was missing two pieces. Goofy's head and Minnie's legs were nowhere to be found, and I had to relinquish it. If you are a fellow puzzler, you know that a puzzle with missing pieces is meaningless and downright cruel.

Creativity was a big part of my life as well. My grandmother had taught me to sew simple stitches. One of my fondest memories is sitting at my Gran's feet with her sewing scraps and mismatched old rhinestone buttons. I would create little square doll pillows and small purses from them. Creativity was a gift that I found great satisfaction in. After completing those little pillows and rhinestone embellished accessories, I would give away my creations to those around me. Gift-giving was my love language from a young age. It gave me joy to make others smile.

And then there was music – a deep part of my soul. I did not care what genre it was; I loved it all. Back then, record players were popular. (I will let you do the math on that one.) There were two songs I remember well. One was by Rick Dees and was titled "Disco Duck." I would encourage you to look that one up on YouTube and experience the goodness for yourself. Despite the tremendous inspirational value of that song, there was one record I would play over and over in my grandmother's kitchen. It was a Bill and Gloria Gaither album with a song called "I'm Something Special." The chorus of this song talks about how God made each of us special and gave us a purpose in life that only we can fulfill. My grandmother encouraged me to get up in front of her little, small-town Baptist church to sing this song in front of everyone, and I did. It was scary and uncomfortable to take on such a request, but I wanted to make my grandmother proud, so I stepped out of my comfort zone that evening. The smile on her face made it all worthwhile. Her happiness made me happy.

Before writing this book, I had forgotten this memory. However, looking back, I can see how God was ministering to me through music before I knew He was there with me. He knew I was struggling with the very words I was singing.

Liar, Liar

At this point in my story, I want to say that there is an enemy of this broken world. He is a thief. God's Word tells us in John 10:10, "The thief comes only to steal and kill and destroy..." and he preys on the young and vulnerable. I was a prime candidate.

I do not like giving the enemy too much credit for everything that happens. We live in a broken and sinful world, and because of that sin, bad things happen. This brokenness was not the plan God had in mind when He created us initially. However, I do not want to dismiss the fact that he is real and has one agenda. Even as a little girl this real enemy had begun to steal from me.

You see, a dark cloud was continuously hanging over my young head. From the outside looking in, my life looked normal. Had you been able to see behind the curtain, you would have seen a dark secret I kept locked away from everyone around me. I was being sexually abused by an older family member. It started around the age of five. I did not tell anyone; I kept it all tucked inside. I was a quiet child and did not speak my mind much. Even when my mother approached me and asked if anything was going on I responded, "No, ma'am." While I wanted to say something on the inside, it just would not come out when I opened my mouth to speak.

People often ask, "Why didn't you tell someone?" My best answer to that question would be that I was protecting others. My abuser had never asked me not to tell or threatened me with anything, yet I felt that if I told, he would be in a lot of trouble and upset with me. The last thing I wanted was for him to be upset with me. Although I did not like the abuse, I loved the fact that he wanted me to come over and play. In my mind, the uncomfortable times were worth the feeling of belonging. This emotion would begin an unhealthy cycle of people-pleasing that would need to be addressed later in my life.

I was also protecting my parents. They were struggling with brokenness in their marriage, and as many children do, I took it upon myself to do the best job I could of not adding to the burden of their struggles. They did not ask for this protection from me. I just wanted them to be happy. As a little girl, I thought I could be that for both of my parents. That was not realistic.

As a result of the abuse, I became extraordinarily distant and shy and learned not to trust others around me. I was perfectly content with my head in a book. Not only did I not have to talk to anyone, but books allowed me to create a different story than the one I was living. Isolation is a place where the enemy likes to keep you. In this place, you are more apt to believe the lies he will begin to feed you.

The enemy loves to feed us lies and con us into believing they are 100% true. When we start to believe these lies as truth, we begin to build a false identity from this. As we focus on the false identity that looks so authentic at the time, we begin to forget who we are. Our true, God-given identity gets buried deep beneath the lies.

For example, one day, as I was with my abuser, an adult in charge walked by the window, saw the abuse, and kept walking. That day, I heard several lies loud and clear: *You are not important. You are not worth saving.*

Looking back now, I realize that was the last time the abuser was alone with me, so even though the caregiver did not bring it to anyone's attention, she had stopped it from happening again.

Regardless, all I could see was what was in front of me now. The song God was singing over me, the song that told me I was something special, slowly faded from my ears. The lie became louder.

This lie would stay with me for many years to come. It spoke loudly into decisions made and actions taken. It would begin forming a false identity of who I truly was.

School Days

Summer ended as school began, and that was never my favorite. Being so shy and not trusting of others, it was hard for me to make friends. My teachers and peers misunderstood me. Remember the lie of *you are not important*? That lie grew into a giant, and the enemy would continue to add to it as often as he could. Coupled with the right circumstances, these lies would be solidified in my brain as truth.

One such circumstance was in second grade. My stomach had been upset that morning, but I did not want to get up and ask the teacher to go to the bathroom. The point came when I felt like I could not hold it any longer, and I had to get up and ask permission to go. As I approached her desk, not wanting my peers to hear me ask, I leaned over and whispered, "I have to go to the bathroom; I can't hold it." She refused me, saying the bell was about to ring and I could go at that time. Reluctantly, I went back to my seat to wait for the bell to ring, which seemed like an eternity.

The minute the bell rang, I started walking down the long sidewalk toward the bathroom. If you have ever experienced that walk to the bathroom where you are trying to hold it in, you know what I mean when I say the faster I walked, the longer the sidewalk seemed to extend. I did not make it in time. As I stepped over the threshold of the girl's bathroom door, I had poop running down the legs of my pants. I was mortified. Trying my best to clean myself up, it was a losing battle. Giving up, I sat on the toilet and cried until someone went and told another teacher who knew me. She came in to help. I will forever be grateful for her; she was an angel and comforted me, even though I am confident it took all she had to keep that loving smile on her face. I went home early that day with the lie ringing in my little head: *No one will listen to you; your voice does not matter because you are not important.*

The following school year, this lie continued to follow me. I would not speak up and ask for help if I did not understand the classwork. *Why should I? No one was going to listen anyway.* The lie from the previous year had formed this belief into my identity already. I remember having to stand at the chalkboard for an entire recess because I would not count the coins placed on the board and write the total amount they equaled. It was not that I would not; I could not. I did not understand the concept of money. Standing there staring at the coin pictures taped to the board, I was embarrassed and devastated. All my classmates had their turn and did it with such ease.

They left for recess with me standing at the board and returned from break with me still staring at the board. I felt like a dunce as I fought back the tears and commanded them not to fall. The teacher might as well have put one of those big cone hats on me with a sign that said, "Everyone knows Angie is dumb and bad at math." However, she did not have to. The enemy made it very clear in my mind when he fed me that familiar lie of *you are not important* with a twist of *you are not smart. You are especially not good at math.*

Hope For The Hurting

Our identities begin to form during the early years. Many things we struggle with today in our adult life can be traced back to hurts from our childhood that need the healing and restorative touch of the Savior. The good news is that He can bind up those wounds, care for us as we heal, and restore all the enemy has stolen. The rest of John 10:10 says, "...I came so that they would have life, and have it abundantly." I am living proof of this promise. Many other women I have walked with, mentored, and ministered to can also attest to His promise. So, if you are reading this book, have hope. He will do the same for you, my friend.

Over the years of healing and restoration, God has graciously walked me through many things. Many of them have been hard lessons. At times, as with the previous stories, it has been challenging to revisit memories from the past that I had swept under the rug. Convincing myself that *those are things everyone goes through, no big deal*, I could forget them and move on. These thoughts were lies in themselves. This is where He began to show me how the truth can come in and set you free. Time and again, when something came up in my life, He would show me the root of that wound from the past. The greatest thing about it is that He does not show you the wound to take you back to victimhood. On the contrary, He takes you back to completely dig up the root so you can live in complete freedom. Freedom is possible.

To accept this freedom, we must first accept the freedom giver. His name is Jesus. He is the foundation we can begin to build our identity on.

As I mentioned earlier, as a little girl, I was given parents who loved me and raised me in church, trying to teach me about this foundation. I say "trying" because I was hearing with my ears but not hearing with my heart. I knew God was real and that He had sent His Son to die for me. I also believed that the Word of God was the truth. That was all head knowledge without putting it all into a relational perspective. In my mind, I saw God as a dictator who sat on His throne in heaven and would only respond when you did something wrong. He was watching for opportunity to punish you. That was not a relationship. Therefore, I did not pursue it as such. I tried to follow all the rules and check off the boxes on my list to stay in His good graces. This is called religion. What I needed was a relationship.

This relationship cannot be given to you by anyone else, as much as they may want you to have it. It is very personal between you and God. My parents did a fantastic job introducing me to Him, yet this was something I would have to choose to nurture and grow on my own.

It was not until much later in my life, when I hit rock bottom, when I would begin to find this relationship by reading His Word in an entirely different way. What was different? I began searching for Him with my whole heart. Only then did all the pieces of my broken and shattered heart fall into place like those beloved puzzles. As He began to place each piece into its rightful place, I began to see the picture clearly of who He was and, in turn, see myself through His eyes.

As I have mentored women over the years, I have seen how most women do not start to look for that deep healing relationship until after they have tried everything else, it has failed them, and they are desperate for change. That is precisely what happened in my story. Although we may have made it much harder on ourselves than it had to be, the great news is that He is ready to restore all that has been stolen from us. He is a God of restoration, healing, and hope. His love never fails.

If you have never accepted Jesus into your life, there is no better time than the present. It is not a complicated formula. As you will see in my story, He does not require us to be perfect to come to Him. That is one of the most remarkable characteristics I have learned about

Him. He is loving and kind and will accept us where we are right now, mess and all. Once we know more about Him and fall in love with the Creator Himself, we will begin to see our hearts change to draw closer to Him. He will never force us into something for which we are not ready. If you want to do that now, say this prayer aloud. He is here, listening to you now.

"Lord, I acknowledge now that I want more for my life than I have been living. Come into my life and my heart and heal the broken places. I invite You to help me. I invite You to show me Your love and who You are. I want to know You more."

I encourage you to get to know who God truly is and build a loving relationship with Him. As we journey together through my story, I will share how I came to know Him and how you can begin your journey of getting to know a love like no other. My life forever changed because of my love story with Him, and I want you to experience it too.

If you already know Him, I hope my story invites you into a deeper love for Him. There is always more to be received because His love is so deep and never ending.

2

Hearing

Before moving forward in our story, it is vital for us to talk about the different ways that God can speak to us. We will be seeking answers from Him throughout this journey, and we need to know how to hear those answers.

Jeremiah 33:3 is one of my favorite promises in the Bible. It says, "Call to Me and I will answer you, and I will tell you great and mighty things, which you do not know."

First, know that God wants to speak to us. He longs to have a personal relationship. He wants us to call out to Him so He can tell us the things we do not know. It delights His heart to hear His daughters call out to Him. Just as He loved walking and talking to Adam and Eve in the garden, He still wants that kind of friendship with us.

Second, we do not have to learn how to get God to speak to us; we must learn how to listen to hear what He is *already* saying. As you learn how God speaks, you will begin to realize He has been speaking to you all along. Like anything else in life, learning to hear God's voice requires a little practice. The more you practice hearing God's voice, the better you will become at it. Once you learn, you will hear the most amazing things. You will find peace in knowing you are not alone in this life. He is always just a whisper away.

He speaks to us in multiple ways, and those ways may change as we change and grow. He may even use various ways on a given day, so be open to all of them.

The Truth Shall Set You Free

The primary way God speaks to us is through His Word. Romans 10:17 says, "So faith comes from hearing, and hearing by the word of Christ."

Hebrews 4:12 tells us, "For the word of God is living and active..." It is not just a good storybook written by men. The Word is given to us by a God alive and active today. As we read His words from long ago, He is breathing life into them for our here and now.

By reading His Word, we learn who He is, who we are, and how to continually apply His Word to our lives to grow closer to Him. It is vital that we are in the Word and reading it daily to increase our hearing and understanding.

There are so many Bible apps out there now that break down the Bible into sections for you to read through the Bible in a year. My favorite one is called "The Bible Recap with Tara-Leigh Cobble." Its companion podcast also explains what you have read for that day in an easy-to-understand commentary. I have learned so much about God and His love for me by taking 30 minutes each morning to enjoy His Word through this amazing program. As if that is not enough, it's free too! Visit thebiblerecap.com to learn how to get started.

Knowing His Word makes it easier to replace the lies that have tormented us for so long. We learn what He says and take them as our truths. John 8:31-32: "So Jesus was saying to those Jews who had believed Him, 'If you continue in My word, then you are truly My disciples; and you will know the truth, and the truth will set you free.'" I am sure you will agree with me in saying I want the truths that will set me free. I am tired of all the false truths I have been fed from this world. Those false truths, aka lies, have kept me down for way too long. When I need to know that what I am hearing with my human ears is truth, I always take it to His Word. If it lines up with what He says, it is 100% true, and I can take it to the bank.

Sweet Dreams

I have had experience hearing from God in several other ways. My favorite way of hearing God speak to me is through dreams. These dreams are always very detailed. When I wake up, I remember colors, smells, small details of clothing, conversation, and the surroundings. Creative people tend to hear from Him this way often. I jokingly say that He chooses this form of communicating with me because it is the only time I am quiet enough to listen without talking back. I can be stubborn at times. (Do not tell my husband I admitted to that.)

Whenever I have dreams like this, I always write them in my dream journal. Many times, after waking up, I may think *this dream was just craziness; there is no way it has any meaning.* Later, something will happen or something will be said to prompt me to go back and look through my dream journal. More often than not, I have been surprised to see God speaking to me through those crazy dreams, and now it all makes sense.

I am not going to lie...some dreams make me question my sanity, while others that I know are from Him immediately make me question His!

This book was a result of such hearing. As I woke up from my slumber, the dream started forming in my memory, and I laughed aloud. "That's funny, God." It was a simple dream. No storyline went along with it. It was just a book. A book with a catchy title and my name stamped at the bottom. Right then, I decided it was not from

God, and I was NOT writing that one down in my dream journal. I reminded God of the struggles I encountered with writing a simple three-page essay for college English classes and how I would cry each time I had to write one. *There is no way I can attempt an entire book. Besides that, I do not have a thing to write. In addition, only smart intellectual people write books. I am more of a free spirit. I could belt out some poetry or something. Maybe one of those limerick-style poems, but only one, not an entire book.*

That was a perfect example of the stubbornness I was referring to. I have argued with God a lot. Yet, He is patient with me each time as I finally come around to accept that He's always accurate. In my defense, I have not only learned how to say "yes" more but at a faster speed than before. As we all are, I am a work in progress. Thank you, Lord, for being patient with me as I learn to trust that You will never lead me somewhere alone. You will be right there beside me.

Singing Over Me

God can also speak to you through music. I love music. He loves music. "The Mighty One, will save; He will rejoice over you with gladness, He will quiet you with His love, He will rejoice over you with singing." (Zephaniah 3:17 NKJV). This verse paints such a beautiful picture. So many times, as I searched for His counsel, comfort, and joy, I would hear just the right song playing that spoke directly to my heart and soul.

There have been several times, also, when I have woken up with a song playing in my head. I would Google the words to find the name of it so I could go and listen. At first, I'd think *wow, that was a great song*, but I soon realized the songs would always be significant to me for the day or season I was walking through. He was singing over me. He is singing over you too, my friend.

Whispers of Love

His still, small voice is another way He can speak to you. God is so gentle and loving. He is such a gentleman. Gentlemen do not yell; they whisper into your ear and down into your soul.

You may be praying about something, and you start to feel in your heart that you already know what to do. That is the still small voice of the Holy Spirit. Some people compare it to our conscience. When you lean into that feeling being the answer to your inquiry, you get peace in your spirit.

Impressions can be whispers too. You may be sitting there, and a picture of something or somebody drops quietly into your mind. You were not thinking about that subject; it just came out of nowhere. Similarly, He may suddenly drop an idea, word, or phrase into your mind.

Impressions and the still small voice are the easiest to dismiss and tell yourself, "That wasn't God, that was just me." No worries. Fortunately, God is patient and does not mind repeating things to us. So, if you miss it the first time, He may speak the same thing to you again, but differently. This is confirmation, which can come in a variety of ways. The more you realize God is speaking, the less you will need extra confirmation to act on what He is telling you. Yet, it always makes me smile when He confirms things to me.

Say it Again

I needed a lot of confirmation as I wrestled with Him in writing this book. The first confirmation came through a special friend from my past who I had not stayed connected with over the years. Our paths crossed on Facebook when I posted about my little girl's dog passing away. She replied to my post with sympathy and asked for my address to send my daughter a special gift. I gladly sent it to her and was extremely touched by her kindness. However, I was not expecting what came to my mailbox four days later. It was a set of children's chapter books that she had written.

Why was I surprised? Until then, I had not told anyone about my book dream or the struggle I was having with it. Even after receiving the books she sent, it took me another month to reach out to her on the subject. My message was as follows: "Hypothetically speaking, what if one thought that God was giving someone stories and lessons about their journey and asking them to write them all down and hinting to this person that they might need to publish these stories? What advice would you give?"

As you can tell from that message, I still did not own the assignment given to me. She was very encouraging with her advice to me. She replied, "Write everything down. God will send someone to help you organize them later. Just pour out on paper what He pours in your heart. It is time. Obedience, not perfection, is His desire."

This answer was more confirmation. That was not the first time this phrase had been said to me over the past few weeks. "Obedience, not perfection..." God does that for us. He will repeat what He is trying to get us to hear as many times as it takes for us to truly listen. He had been working in my heart about

wanting things to be done perfectly before I could move forward. To stall my obedience, my excuse was *I am not good* (perfect) *at writing.* He was inviting me to examine the pain of perfect performance to give me healing, which would ultimately lead to freedom. He knew I could not move fully into my calling with the weight of seeking perfection in my life.

I wish I could say I sat right down and began writing my story. I wish

I could say that I immediately gave over my burden of perfection to Him. However, I am 100% vulnerable in this book to you. I must confess to you that I did neither one! I continued to wrestle with the assignment He called me to do, holding on to the excuse that I was not a writer. I was not perfected in writing, as evidenced by my past; therefore, *I could not possibly write an entire book.*

So, what did He do? He sent more confirmation. Fast forward 16 months. I attended a business conference where I was learning new marketing skills for my business. I was creating a company to help women find employment after leaving the sex trade industry or the prison system.

When I was talking to a fellow attendee whom I had just recently gotten to know, she paused mid-sentence and gave me the strangest look. I looked back at her smiling and asked, "What? Why are you looking at me like that?" She simply said, "Oh, nothing." She smiled back, shook her head, and finished her sentence. We enjoyed each other's company and became chair neighbors for the rest of the conference.

Toward the end of the conference, we were assigned to write down one goal we would commit to achieving in the next six months. For 16 months, I had continued to wrestle with this book writing. I had not once sat down to even attempt to write. I could hear God telling me to start and always found a way to feel okay with blocking Him out. As I was thinking about what to write on this blank paper staring back at me, I could hear that still small voice telling me, "Now would be the perfect time to commit to writing your book."

One thing you should know about me: When I make a solid commitment to something, I do it. That is part of my reason for denying this assignment in the first place. I knew that if I embraced it and committed my mind and heart to it, I would have no choice but to pursue it.

With fear in my heart, I quickly wrote the words, "I will have the first draft of my book finished in the next six months." I had NO CLUE if that was even possible. I did not know the first thing about writing a book. The only thing I knew was that I was tired of running from my assignment. I wanted to be obedient to my Father, so I quickly ran to the back table to turn it in before changing my mind. Sitting back in my chair, I looked straight ahead, letting it all sink in. *What the heck did I just do?*

After the session was over, we broke for lunch. I joined my new friend and chair neighbor, Sandi, and some other members at a nearby restaurant. They were all talking about the goals we had just written down. I was hesitant to share mine but decided to break through the fear and just spill it. I went on to explain that I had no clue how to write a book, didn't even know what the book was supposed to be about, and all I had was a book title that God gave me in a dream over two years ago.

Sandi replied, "Well, at least you have the title. I am in the process of writing my book, and I don't have a title yet." Sandi was writing a book of her own. Of course, she was. *I see how you set me up here, Lord. Clever indeed. I see what You did!*

Returning to the conference room, Sandi looked at me again, smiling. She then said, "Remember earlier when you asked me why I was looking at you like I was?" "Yes," I replied. "Well, I was talking to you, and when I looked at your face, I saw the word "Author" written across your forehead." We both laughed. God will often use others to communicate His message to you, as He did with Sandi.

And so began my journey as an author. Never would I have thought I would type that in a sentence...in a book...my own book! Co-written with God.

His Plans Are Best

I continued to struggle as I sat down to write. This time it was over the content. I had a book title; however, I was still wrestling with *what exactly would you have me write, Lord?* I began to pray each time before opening the laptop, asking Him to give me the words He wanted you to hear as you read my book. I would start typing, and the words would begin to flow into my mind and onto the page. See how that works? He is now using impressions to speak to me to speak to you through the words of this book.

It did not always flow perfectly. My perfectionist tendencies got in my way time after time. I wanted to know what the final product would look like as I navigated through naming chapters and writing the content. I wanted Him to speak to me and tell me everything up front so I could write better. There I go again, telling God how the plan should play out. You will see throughout my story I do this an embarrassingly large number of times.

Yet, I already knew this is not how God works. First, if I had all the answers right up front, I would be relying on my strength and knowledge, not His. Isaiah 55:9 reminds us, "For as the heavens are higher than the earth, so are My ways higher than your ways and my thoughts than your thoughts." God's thoughts and ideas are always better than mine.

Second, the chances are great that if He revealed everything He had planned for me right up front, it would completely overwhelm me, causing me to shut down and quit immediately. I know I would have. As I have written my story and prepared it for the editor, thinking I was finished, He has shown me that what I have is meant for not one book but two. So, be looking for the next one soon.

Life is a journey of growth. He walks alongside us as we learn the lesson meant for each day. As we understand that lesson, we can take another step of faith into the next lesson. We can only do this with Him. We were never meant to walk it out alone. As I reflect on how far I have come in this writing journey, I see it all too well. Had He revealed everything to me the morning after the dream occurred, I would have shut Him down and packed it tightly away, never to emerge again. Instead, He was patient and gentle. He slowly spoke things to me as I was ready to listen. He placed people in my path at just the right moment with confirmation I needed to encourage and guide me. He is good like that.

Speaking Through the Trials

As I finished the final review of my story and got it ready for print, I had to come back and add something here. As I have mentioned, this book was a healing journey. If you have not recognized what was happening in the big book-writing struggle, let me help you see. The lies I had been fed as a little girl still surfaced at the age of 49. Although I had healed from a considerable amount of heart wounds created in my past, this one was still showing up strong. As I was arguing with God, thoughts quickly came pouring in, saying, *you are not smart enough to write a book. No one wants to hear your story; your voice does not matter. You are not that important.*

At the time, I was still not seeing clearly; the lies were holding me down. I honestly believed the arguments I was posing were 100% accurate. To see the lies would mean I had to walk down some hard roads again through memories I had already packed up.

This brings me to my last point in hearing God. He will speak healing words to us through the trials in our lives. Often, we can learn some deep things He wants to speak to us through our trials. Rarely do we welcome these with open arms, and we might even view them as punishment. That is not God's way. He may allow us to walk some challenging roads, but it is always about His love for us. Furthermore, as we are walking in those hard places, He is walking alongside us. He is patiently and lovingly waiting for us to invite Him to heal those dark places, to open our eyes to the lies so we can lay them down forever at His feet.

As I have been obedient to sit down and write this book, I have seen the lies I was still holding close. Typing these words out just now brings tears of healing that are flowing down my face. He knows what we need so much more than we do. I needed to obey Him because there was healing waiting for me in my obedience.

He knows when we are ready to receive the healing too. It is always in His timing, and although His timing is not ours, His timing is always right on time.

He brings me more profound healing each day as I share my story with you. Slowly, the lies are being replaced with His truth of what I am capable of being and doing. He was there all along, wanting to walk me into the truth I had buried deep under the lies from my past. Thank you, Lord, for not giving up on me when You knew what I needed. And thank you for being with me as I leaned into the hard things to find more freedom.

Always Growing

As I have grown in my listening to His voice, I have learned to have back-and-forth conversations with Him. I ask a question, and He answers. This can happen in several different ways. Sometimes, when I ask a question, I will immediately have an impression drop into my mind. Other times, He will reveal the answer to me over time in the ways we previously discussed. Whatever way He chooses to answer, the critical thing to remember is that He is always listening and working.

There are places where I can meet with God that bring me greater clarity to hear Him. Nature is a prominent place, especially near the water. Near our home, there is a park with a lake with a walking path around it. The lake has ducks, geese, blue herons, turtles, and many singing frogs. I will drive there on pretty days, put on my praise and worship music, and walk around the lake. I can truly feel God walking right next to me. We have had some of our most significant conversations here.

Certain activities will draw us closer to God too. As a jewelry designer, I find that when I am creating something with my hands, His voice is heard more clearly. My opinion for why this happens is that as I create something from nothing; I am imitating Christ, who was the first Creator. When we imitate someone, we become more like them. As I become more like Christ, I am able to hear His voice better.

Although those are just some of the more common ways God speaks to us, there are hundreds more. Our God is so personal. He knows how we best hear Him and will speak to us individually. He knows us better than anyone because He created us.

Practicing hearing from God will continue until the day we leave this world. We are continually growing in this area. Never quit listening. I cannot wait to hear of all the different ways He speaks to you and all the great things He will tell you, my friend.

3

Doors to the Heart

Growing up, my grandfather was highly skilled with his hands. He was a carpenter and a painter. He had built the house where he and Gran lived. There were several doors on the house that he had also designed and built.

Walking through the front door of Gran's house was always a warm and welcoming feeling. She had a gift for hospitality and could make anyone feel loved behind her doors. Many families and friends walked through that front door which led straight into her kitchen. She always had something sweet cooked and the old percolating coffee pot ready to brew a hot cup.

There was another door rarely used by visitors that led from the living room to the backyard. That door held many memories for me. It had a window overlooking the backyard where many of my childhood memories would bloom like the flowers Gran and I planted there.

I would host tea parties for my stuffed animals and baby dolls in that yard as my Gran looked out the door to check on me. Outside this door is the back porch where I would practice dance moves that would get me discovered one day for the big stage. This door would be my lookout point as I snuck to see where the Easter eggs were being hidden so I could get a jump on my older cousin when the hunt's "ready, set, go" was announced.

Although this door held so many great memories for me, it also contained some that were not so great. One that stands out involves a college girl from our church. She had told me on Sunday that she would pick me up at Gran's house and take me out for ice cream on Tuesday. I was so excited. I liked this girl. She talked to me and really listened when I had something to say. I got dressed early in the day, waited by that door, and looked out often, anticipating her arrival any minute. Gran must have known at some point that she was not coming, as she kept trying to coax me away from the door to sit down and eat something. I assured her, "No. I can't eat; I'm going out for ice cream." She never came. Again, the lie screamed at me: *You are not important. You are easily forgotten.*

Doors serve many purposes. They can welcome people in or shut people out. They can be locked in protection to either keep things out or keep things in. There are also many different types of doors, from decorative doors with lots of windows to solid-steel doors with no windows.

Like those physical doors, we have spiritual doors protecting our hearts. They, too, can either serve the purpose of keeping people out or welcoming them in. They can be doors full of beautiful windows that allow us to see the beauty of those around us and enable people to see the beauty inside of us. Or they can be the cold, dark, solid steel doors nothing can penetrate.

My spiritual doors had once been beautifully designed, pristine white, with rounded tops, windows from top to bottom, and a jeweled crystal knob for a handle. The summer sun would shine brightly through the crystal-clear windows as I viewed the world on the other side with hope and a future.

However, as the sexual abuse continued in my young life, the sun began to fade. The first abuser would move on, but many more would take his place. The beautiful white paint on my spiritual doors started to crack, peel, and fall off, leaving them susceptible to the outside elements.

The crystal-clear glass window of my doors began to turn dark and ugly, covered in film that prevented me from seeing the outside world as it was. I had fallen hook, line, and sinker for the lies that hissed *you are not important.*

I began boarding up the spiritual doors to my heart one by one. This would ensure that no one could pick the lock and walk in without permission. I did not trust myself to know who to allow into the doors of my heart, so it was best to just shut everyone out. I had been deceived for so long by people I thought I could trust, only to find out they were not trustworthy. This was my way of protecting myself from further hurt.

Shutting doors to your heart feels like protection, yet it only leads you further into isolation. As we have pointed out, this is where the enemy will keep you as he persuades you into believing more lies. *You cannot tell anyone else how you are feeling, they would not understand. They will laugh at you. You are the only one going through this.* Thoughts like this will spill into your mind, and eventually take root in your heart.

Knock, Knock – Nobody's Home

Like I mentioned, I had serious trust issues. This door, "trust," was completely torn down and replaced with a cold, dark, solid-steel door and locked up tight with a key. My trust door would remain barricaded for a long time. It would also be the last door to be reopened to allow God's healing light back in. To do this, I would have to invite Him in and reopen those doors as He walked with me on a restoration journey. Together, we would rebuild trust to grant the appropriate people access to my heart.

All that sounds so beautiful, right? Inviting Him in to shine light into the dark places and restoring me to allow people to get close again. The words drip with roses and sunshine. But it was not attractive at all during the process. Those hinges had been rusted shut. To even begin to open those closed doors was painful. It was intense and scary. My flesh wanted to stay behind the closed-off door where I was convinced that I was secure from the pain of being hurt by others. I could not even trust Him with my heart for the longest time. Unfortunately, He would be the last person to whom I would trust to give my whole heart.

It reminds me of my little girl after she fell and scraped her knee. As her mom, I want to clean it up, get the dirt and debris out, cover it with healing medicine, and secure it with a protective bandage. She fought me the entire time, saying, "It will hurt. Do not touch it." She is correct. It does hurt while getting it clean and protected; however, letting it get infected will hurt *much* more in the long run.

We are much like that with Jesus. Psalm 147:3 tell us, "He heals the brokenhearted and binds up their wounds." That is what He wants to do for us. Yet, we are fighting Him the entire time, crying out, "No! Do not touch that one. It will hurt too much. I am not ready yet." So, by our choices, we allow the door to stay closed and the wound to keep growing until it is infected.

It took me years to give in and face the fact that I needed a new heart, totally renewed by Him. I wish I had allowed Him in sooner, but thankfully, there is good news: if you are still breathing, He can deliver. Thank you, Lord, for meeting me where I was and providing the healing my heart needed.

Ezekiel 36:26: "Moreover, I will give you a new heart and put a new spirit within you; and I will remove the heart of stone from your flesh and give you a heart of flesh."

His Gifts

Although I lost my trusting heart as a child, I never lost the softness. There was never a time when I remember being bitter over the things that were happening to me, nor to those who hurt me. I thank God for that. I recently asked Him, "How did this door of a soft heart withstand through my younger years?" As we have discussed, when we ask, He will answer. In answering my question, He revealed three gifts He had given me as a little girl.

Gift #1

One was the gift of imagination. Riding the school bus, sitting alone in my seat with my head leaned against the cold window, I would take myself to another place. I would visualize myself on a gorgeous white horse with a flowing mane and tail, riding the wind, imagining all the kids on the bus watching me ride as they looked on through the bus windows. They were not jealous; I was not prideful. They were celebrating me.

I imagined the desires of my heart. These desires were to be seen, celebrated, and to experience freedom. As I look back on that memory, it was the Holy Spirit speaking to me before I truly knew. He was the one celebrating me and telling me I was important, seen, and heard. He kept that desire burning so I would not lose complete hope of achieving it.

Today, I still hold on to this gift. As a jewelry designer and entrepreneur, it comes in handy to imagine something that has yet to be seen.

Most children possess the gift of imagination through play. Looking back, what things did you often imagine as a child? Can you see some of those ideas playing out in your life now?

Gift #2

The second was the gift of creativity. I was always creating something with cloth, paper, crayons, clay, or whatever I could lay my hands on. I loved drawing and painting, building with Legos, crochet, cross-stitch, and building imaginary villages out of sticks and acorns. If I could think it, I could create it. He is the Great Creator. We are made in His image. He has woven Himself into all of us in many ways. For those of us He has gifted with this skill, when we create with our hands, there is a release of His goodness that flows out like a therapeutic medicine.

As we have walked this healing journey together, He has shown me that He not only placed the gifts of imagination and creativity within me to help me through my hard times, but He knew I would use them later to bring others through their healing journey into restoration. Each person has a type of creativity. Maybe yours isn't crafts, sewing, or drawing, but without a doubt I know God has gifted you with things you are good at. What skills come naturally to you? What activities give you peace when you do them?

Gift #3

The third was the gift of an earthly father who modeled a soft heart and compassion for others for me. One memory that stands out is my 4th-grade year of school. My class was playing in a kickball tournament.

Side note – Kickball was *not* one of my gifts, and I hated being picked for team sports. Who thought that was a great idea? I was always the last to be selected. Talk about self-esteem wounds. I could write another entire book on just that subject. In art, you never had to pick teams. Everyone's creation was a winner. I vote for art and creativity any day!

Anyway, I did not have a choice not to play that day since it was a class-wide event for physical education. My dad had come to watch us play. I am sure it was out of pure love and not for entertainment value. While watching, he noticed a little boy in my class with worn out shoes and pants that were too short. He asked me some questions about him that night at home. The only thing I knew about him was that he was poor, and the other kids made fun of him a lot. My dad must have also talked with the teacher, because over the weekend, we went shopping. Together we picked out several pairs of pants, some shirts, socks, and shoes. We skipped the underwear aisle at my request.

It was a week before Christmas break. My mom, who modeled the gift of creativity for me, helped wrap all the items in several boxes with festive, colorful paper, and handmade bows. The plan was for Dad to drop the gifts anonymously at the school office, where the boy's mother would pick them up.

It felt so exhilarating to be a part of a secret mission. That played very well into my imaginative spirit.

I will never forget the first day back to school after the holiday break. As I was sitting at my desk waiting for class to start, he walked in wearing one of the outfits I had picked out. Seeing him walk to his desk with a more confident air that day made me smile from ear to ear.

Later that school year, this same boy stole something special from me. I was hurt, but I never retaliated. I was not bitter or angry. I kept that soft and forgiving heart. Thank you, Lord, for the gifts that You give.

Some of the gifts we possess have been passed down from our family, either genetically or by learned behaviors. Think about the gifts and talents you have received from people in your life. What are they? As you think of things, remember to celebrate that person in your life for the impact they made.

Not All Doors Are Meant to Open

There is one more door I want to discuss before closing out this chapter. It was a door that had been opened and should not have been. It was a door meant to stay shut until I was mature enough to handle what was behind it. As it was continuously being forced open, I tried to close it and lock it back up, but I was not strong enough. This was the door of "purity."

Doors that are not meant to be opened can be opened in two different ways: either by people or circumstances beyond your control or willingly stepping through the door yourself. The first happened to me as a young person, and then the second in the next season of my life. The door had first been opened by my abuser when I was too young to know how to close it. It was not my fault. Once a door has been opened, it is easier to open again and again, as we will see later in my story.

According to Collins Online Dictionary, the word purity is "freedom from anything that contaminates or pollutes." Purity had been taken from me. As a result, I had lost that freedom from contamination and pollution. My heart would become contaminated and confused as I learned about sex and love. My thoughts would be polluted into thinking that one was exchanged for the other. I would spend most of my life searching for love in this way. This would be another long journey to heart healing that would extend well into my adult life. The enemy thought he had a foothold in that door, and he did for a season; however, love always wins. God's love was chasing me. Eventually, it would catch me and never let me go.

My grandmother and grandfather have since passed from this world. We recently tore down their house due to its condition. However, before we did, I had my husband take down that door leading from the living room to the backyard. It was in excellent condition. We were able to clean it up and install it in our new home.

Today, as I stand looking out that same window of that same door, I marvel at His goodness and mercy. I see a life of freedom, grace, and everlasting love. I have learned to trust, know my worth through His eyes, and have given Him complete control over my life and all my days. I often think of the little girl who stood on the other side of life and wish she could have seen what awaited her on the other side.

4

You Can't Judge a Book by Its Cover

Books were my happy place. I would much rather read a good love story than watch television any day. I would pick books where I could put myself as the story's main character. Most love stories start and end the same way with a slight twist in between to make them stand out.

Once upon a time, a beautiful young girl was living her dream. Then, the plot suddenly changes, and she desperately needs a rescuer. The hero swoops in, rescues her, and they live happily ever after. Am I right? Any other love story would not be worth fantasizing about.

I loved all the love stories. *Cinderella* was, and still is, one of my favorites. I could see myself singing, dancing, and talking to all the animals just as she did. She kept her soft heart as she battled with the stepmother and stepsisters. In the end, she is pursued and found by the prince and lives happily ever after. Sigh.

However, my favorite book was *The Little Princess*. I must have read that book at least a dozen times. With flashlight in hand, I would hide under my blanket and read until my eyes would no longer stay open. If you are not familiar with this book, it was about a little girl who had been left at a home for girls by her father as he left for the war. He promised to return for her as soon as the battle ended. Being a high-ranking officer, he was wealthy and had left plenty of money for her to live comfortably at the orphanage. She had a kind heart and befriended several other girls who were unaccepted.

Word comes back from the war that her father is dead. At this point, the orphanage manager takes all her expensive clothes, toys, and furniture and sells them after banishing her to the attic with the scullery girl. It was cold, dark, and empty. She was not given enough food to eat. She teaches the scullery girl how to use her imagination to escape the negative situation. Together at night, they imagine a fancy party with beautiful dresses, table spreads of food, and fine linens and tableware. In the end, she is rescued. I will not tell you how or by who in case you want to read it yourself.

I could relate to the little princess in the story. Although she had a big heart for others, she would be misunderstood by many. I, too, in my preteen years, would be misunderstood. Unlike the main character in my book, I would not stand up for myself. Continuing to allow the enemy's lies to speak loudly, I would persist in believing *my voice does not matter, and no one would listen anyway.*

The Plot Twist

Remember, the first part of John 10:10 states, "The thief comes only to steal and kill and destroy..." He does not want us to accomplish the purpose we were born to walk out. For this reason, he will attack those things the hardest.

Such was the case for my voice. I had already begun to agree with these lies early on, but they would continue to grow more solid in my mind as situations emerged that would set the stage for their authenticity in my heart.

One such stage was presented as my mom was visiting a church friend's home. I always looked forward to playing with the friend's son. We would play outside for hours, climbing trees and hiding in the bushes while stalking the bad guys (aka the neighbors on the other side of the fence). That day, he asked me if I wanted to ride his bicycle around the neighborhood block. Having no sidewalks in the country, only dirt and gravel, I was thrilled at the invitation. This was an exciting and new adventure for me.

Upon returning, he comes running up to me with mischief in his eyes and says, "My dad wants to talk to you!" I knew from the look on his face that it was not good. As I sat down in his father's office chair and looked across the desk, I saw his accusing eyes staring through me. He reprimanded me for taking the bike out of the yard, which was against the house rules. I opened my mouth several times to tell him that I did not know I was breaking any rules. Again, he made it clear that I was guilty, and my voice was not believed. Walking back out, his son was standing in the driveway, holding up his bike with a sly grin on his face.

This same boy would later set me up again. This time we were in his dad's office. He was playing on his dad's computer, and I was creating a masterpiece from a blank piece of paper while lying on the floor. The son beckoned me to the computer to "show me something cool" as he pressed print on the keyboard. I looked at the screen and saw a word I honestly did not know the meaning of. I knew it was not a nice word, and in fact, it was outright forbidden in my household. You know the one. It starts with the same letter as fun. As Yoda would say, "Fun this night would be not."

It all happened so fast. His dad walked into the office to retrieve his pen as the paper was mid-print. The son rips the half-printed paper out of the printer, balls it up, and throws it in the nearby trashcan. I stood there like deer in the headlights with my mouth wide open. His dad leaves the room. I was so scared. I was a rule follower, and I was pretty sure that had to be against their house rules. I gathered my stuff and went to find my mother. I did not tell her anything that had happened, and I honestly did not think about it again because I did not do anything wrong.

On the other hand, not everyone had those same thoughts. My mom was asked to bring me over to talk to his father the next day. I did not know that was our purpose until we walked into their house, and he sat me back down in the oversized, cold leather chair overlooking the same large desk and accusing face. This time the talk included phrases of "habit of breaking the rules" and "if you continue to behave like this." I did not even try to defend myself this time. He would not believe me anyway.

From that point on, I was treated differently. I was looked at as the "bad kid" by this group of church members. I was, indeed, misunderstood.

It should have come as no surprise to me when I confided in those same people after being sexually abused by an older boy in the church, and they asked me, "Angie, are you sure you are telling the truth? He says that he did not do anything to you."

This was the moment the lie would be permanently etched into my identity. *You are not important. You have no voice. No one will ever believe what you have to say.*

Turning the Page

As I was writing this part of my story, I debated on whether to include the fact that the people involved were in our church family. I had even written the chapter and went back to remove it at one point. However, it is essential to note that the enemy also wanted to destroy that part of my life.

So many of us have been hurt by people we were supposed to trust inside the church walls. Somehow, we put a higher value on the hurt when it comes from inside those walls. The truth is, we are all human, the church family included.

As with any family, church or not, we will not always see eye to eye, and we will hurt each other at some point along the way. Humans will fail us every time. Our Lord is the only one who will never hurt us. "And the Lord is the one who is going ahead of you; He will be with you. He will not desert you or abandon you. Do not fear and do not be dismayed." Deuteronomy 31:8

In placing a wedge of resentment inside my heart, I grew distant from the church as a whole and automatically dismissed anything they wanted to tell me. I later became bitter and angry, while further isolating myself from any help any future church family could give me.

I found myself doing the same thing I resented them for doing to me. By judging all churches and their members, I placed them into a category based on what I perceived them to be, without giving them a chance to show me who they truly were. I was quick to shut them out based on hurts from my past. *I will never believe what you have to say because you never believed what I had to say.*

Do you know that old saying, "Hurt people, hurt people"? That was a cycle I would live out repeatedly as I shut my heart down piece by piece. My heart would grow cold to those around me, even those I loved, as I let unforgiveness take root and grow.

Later in life, as God graciously walked me through a journey of forgiveness with these people in my life, I developed the heart knowledge I would need for the place He was calling me to serve. I can have such deep compassion for women I minister to in the prison system. I can see through the behaviors that landed them there. You do not always see an accurate picture of someone when only looking at outward appearances or behaviors. You must examine their heart.

I do not believe that anything is ever wasted. Even the adverse, hurtful events in our life can be a learning and growing experience for us.

If you are struggling with this kind of hurt in your life, do not let the word "church" throw you into a tailspin. Through my healing journey, God has brought many men and women into my life through the church and other places. We were never meant to walk this life alone. Ask Him to show you where to find your tribe of women that will build you up and encourage you along the path to healing. I cannot imagine what my life would be missing had I not opened the special place in my heart to let these women into my world. Thank You, Lord, for Your gift of healing and forgiveness.

5

Rescue Me

As a teenager, I decided I was tired of my body being taken without permission. It made sense in my young mind that if I gave it freely, I was in charge. Therefore, I would not be so hurt in the process. At 14, I had sex for the first time on my own terms. Misunderstood again, as a teenage girl, I was viewed as "the bad girl" by many. So, I took on that identity and wore it wholeheartedly. I began sleeping around, partying, and doing everything I knew I should not be doing.

Like the little princess in my favorite book, I longed for a rescuer. I was really looking for someone to fulfill that desire of being loved as the princess I wanted to be. This desire to be loved was not wrong. God designed us as women to yearn for that love. Being seen and heard, sought after, and told you are a beautiful treasure is a desire placed by the Creator Himself.

He placed this desire so deeply within us. It is a desire that almost demands to be fulfilled. However, the original design was for us to look to Him to fulfill this yearning with His steadfast love, not the world's definition of love. This is where things start to go badly; as we turn to man to fulfill the desire of love, it never satisfies. Love of a man was never meant to satisfy our deep longing, no matter how hard we try to make it fit into that God-shaped hole.

Boy, did I try!

I started to look for that love in men. I gave my heart away to those who did not know how to handle it. I would get hurt and abused only to move to the next prospective relationship, thinking this would surely be the one I was searching for. I ended up giving all the pieces of my heart away until nothing was left but brokenness.

I would continue this cycle of selling myself for love. That is what I thought love was – an exchange. In exchange for sex, I would get attention. Attention equated to being seen, being wanted, and belonging. This had to be love. So why does it hurt so bad?

Why did I continually feel like I was fighting for love and losing the battle? When would my Prince Charming come and sweep me off my feet?

My hope was sparked one day as the football quarterback, who sat behind me in typing class, struck up a conversation. It was homecoming week of my Sophomore year in high school; he asked me if I wanted to attend the dance with him. At first, I was suspicious, as he had never talked to me before. Despite noticing the girl sitting next to him was snickering as he sweet-talked me, I ignored all the warning signs and believed this was my big break. I should have seen it coming, as the girl was one of his good friends. But when you are looking for a rescuer, you will fall for a deceiver every time. I was searching so desperately.

We exchanged phone numbers. He even called me the night before to tell me where to meet him on the night of the dance. I could not sleep that night, dreaming about how it would be, imagining us talking and laughing as we danced the night away. He would introduce me to his popular friends, where I would finally be seen and known, as I would be accepted into their elite circle. It was too good to be true.

You know what they say…

As I walked into the high school gym, I spotted my date. He was slow dancing with another girl. When he saw me walk in, he came over and pulled me onto the dance floor to finish the song. The entire time he was being extremely sexually inappropriate. As I struggled to keep his hands off me, he kept looking over my shoulder and laughing. As I turned around, I saw all his friends standing in a group laughing at his behavior. It was then when I realized that it was all a setup.

I was humiliated. I had to face them every Monday, Wednesday, and Friday for the rest of the school year in typing class. Over the clicking of the old-fashioned typewriters, I could plainly hear the taunts and snickers directed at me from the seat directly behind me. This was not the laughter I had imagined in my daydreams. That school year could not go by fast enough for me.

Continuing my promiscuity throughout my high school career, I no longer dated any high school boys. I sought the maturity of college men. In my junior year, I fell for a kindhearted guy attending college in our town. He treated me like the princess I had dreamed of for so long. Knowing this was the love I had been seeking, I did not think twice when he proposed to me one night during my senior year.

Encouraging me to go to college, we started planning for our future. Growing up, I had not thought about my future in a career. My plans were always to get married and have children. However, I wanted to make him happy; therefore, I enrolled in business college.

Let the Performance Begin

After high school graduation, I moved out and started attending the business college in a neighboring town 32 miles from my tiny hometown. Big ideas of getting my education, getting married and starting a family were at the top of my list. Surely this is what life was all about. Isn't this what every girl dreams of? I spent many months envisioning the beautiful wedding dress, the romantic honeymoon, and the children that would follow to fill my life with love and laughter. If I could hurry up and finish this business college to make him happy, I would be on the way to my happily ever after. Everything would be wonderful.

As I would soon learn, I could not perform myself into happiness. Although I wanted to feel love, it just was not there. There were so many deep wounds and hurts within me that I did not know how to love. It would only take a few weeks of being away from my fiancé for me to fall back into old patterns of familiar ground.

While working part-time at a department store near my apartment, I had attracted the attention of an older co-worker. He knew all the things to say to flatter me before asking me out on a date, to which I accepted. Picking me up at my apartment that Friday night, he told me the date destination was a fun surprise. It should have come as no surprise that we ended up in front of his apartment as he invited me in to get his wallet. All men keep their wallets under the pillow of their bed, right?

At this point, I knew what the expected outcome was to be. I also knew that he would take it if I did not give it to him. Sticking to the promise I made to myself years ago, I would not allow that to happen; therefore, I gave myself up that night without a fight.

After getting what he wanted from me, he stated, "You can get out of my bed now." I asked him to drive me back home, to which he refused. So, as he rolled over and went to sleep, I made myself as comfortable as I could on the floor at the end of his bed – no pillow, no cover.

Lying there thinking about how I had gotten to this point again, the enemy began reminding me of the lies. They were coming at me like a firehose. *You are not important. You will always be known for what you can do. That is why men like you.*

As I cried myself to sleep on the floor that night, I resolved that I would no longer be the victim. No one would ever make me cry again. That was a sign of weakness and vulnerability, and I was not weak. Feeling like I was in control gave me a sense of stability.

Later the next week, I would overhear other co-workers talking about me in the break room. I quickly realized the date was never intended to be an actual date. This guy was a part of a fraternity that had a disgusting challenge: seeing how many girls he could sleep with for that month.

Say Goodbye

When my fiancé visited me the next day, I could not look him in the eye. Emotions of every kind ran through my mind. Shame, confusion, and pain were the biggest. I quickly became distant in our relationship as I quit answering phone calls and rarely spoke when we were together. *He is better off with someone else. Surely, he will realize that soon.*

Continuing to cover the pain with sex, I became involved with another guy at my apartment complex. We partied a lot, and I began to sleep through my business classes. Eventually, I would be dismissed from the school due to failing grades and multiple classes missed.

One morning, my fiancé knocked on my door. I knew he was coming that day and had decided this was the day he needed to see who he was pursuing so he could move forward with his life without me. As the guy I was sleeping with answered the door, it all played out before me. It was cruel on my part, yet I was emotionless. My heart was stone cold.

So, This Is Love?

The relationship with the other guy would continue. One day as we were drinking at my apartment, he would look at me and say, "Our kids are going to have pretty eyes." Romantic, right?

At the age of 18, we married. My dream of having a family and being a mother could now happen. There were many red flags beginning this relationship, yet I thought I could manage them, and this would be my chance for my dreams to come true and live happily ever after. Those red flags became real as I found myself in an abusive marriage. Again, convincing myself that it was not that bad and I could control it by performing and doing more of the "only thing I was good at." We were both so young and broken. We each had pasts needing restoration and healing, yet we did not seek that healing.

I gave birth to my first baby girl nine months later. Two years later, her sister was born. They were perfect. Being a mother was more than I had ever imagined. This part of my dream had finally come true. I know that God gave me the gift of my girls to carry me through some hard times. They brought so much joy to my life.

However, I was still looking for the love relationship with a man I was not getting in my current marriage. Often, I blamed myself and thought things would be different *if I could only be a better wife.* I started doing things that I was not comfortable with. In the end, it only left me emptier.

I was still yearning for a rescuer. Yet, I was resolved to the fact that he did not exist, and this was the best life had to offer. Determined to make the best of it, I poured my life into my girls and tried to find my identity in being the best mom I could be for them.

One Day My Prince Will Come

Little did I know that Jesus was waiting so patiently for me. He was waiting for me to put down my sword and quit fighting for the love that was right there. I need only to accept it.

It would still take me a few years to find Him. Continuing to fight, I would have multiple affairs during my 18-year marriage. You see, I was running. I was running from the pain and hurt in my life while not facing the brokenness and disappointments of my past. I looked everywhere to find my identity and purpose in relationships and titles. Something or someone who would validate that I had arrived, was accomplished, and worthy. Mostly, I was looking for happiness in a man.

Happiness is temporary. Joy is eternal. Thank you, Lord, that today You have rescued me and filled me with Your everlasting joy. I no longer walk in sorrow and sighing. You are my rescuer. My Prince...Prince of Peace.

Isaiah 35:10: "And the redeemed of the Lord will return and come to Zion with joyful shouting, and everlasting joy will be on their heads. They will obtain gladness and joy, and sorrow and sighing will flee away."

6

Facing My Giants

As much as I loved being a mother, this identity couldn't carry me through. Children grow up, and they begin to form lives of their own. With my marriage being less than I had hoped for, I began to seek after the love of men again. After multiple affairs didn't produce what I was searching for, I decided to try to go to college and obtain a degree. Perhaps, I could find my fulfillment in a career.

Nursing seemed like something I could enjoy. Besides that, nurses were respected and did important things for the world around them. Surely, this field would give me an identity that I could be proud of. I wanted to prove myself. Outperforming my past would prove to the world that I was important. I wanted to prove that I was smart. I wanted to prove that I was not easily forgotten. I wanted to prove that I was worthy. I wanted to prove that I was good at more than sexual acts. And, yes, I might even be good at math.

Knowing I had struggled with academics in the past, this would be a challenge; however, I was always up for a challenge.

With this determination, I set out to prove to the world who I was. Having no prior college credits, I had to start from the beginning. This included several English and math classes. I wasn't too worried about the English. My love of reading had always pulled me through with pretty good grades in high school English. The math classes worried me, especially after pre-entry testing put me into the remedial class.

I was blessed with an awesome remedial math teacher for my first class. She was key to my success. Taking time with me and listening to my fears, she shared her knowledge with me in a way that made perfect sense. New doors were opened, and her love for math spilled out and over onto me. The day of the first test came up, and I was a nervous wreck. Taking my time to complete it and going back over the entire thing twice, I was the last to turn in my paper. As I walked out the door, I thought, *I probably failed that entire test. It seemed too easy.*

Walking back into the classroom the next day, I knew we would get our test results back. There was a pit in my stomach as the professor started calling our names to pick up our papers. Taking mine back to my desk, I laid it face down and struggled to get the nerve up to turn it over. I could hear my classmates all around me. Some were celebrating, while some were mumbling under their breath in disappointment. I wanted so badly to be in the former group.

My desk was at the front of the row, right in front of the professor's desk. As I looked up at her, she smiled at me as if to say, "It's okay. Look at your test." Taking a deep breath with tears trying to break out from my eyes, I turned it over. The first thing I saw was a big red score of 100%. I couldn't believe what I was seeing. Checking the name at the top of the paper, it looked like my handwriting. Looking back at my professor, she still smiled as I received a thumbs up.

On this day, the lie of *you are not smart* and *you are especially not good at math* began to fade a little. However, it would take a few more test grades for it to sink in that perhaps I am smarter than I once thought, and perhaps I am good at math too.

Math was beginning to become fun and would be one of my best subjects; I found a love for its stability. There was never any guessing. Once you learned the formula, 2 plus 2 would always equal 4.

When the enemy sees you moving into the light, he pays attention. When you begin to thwart his plan for your destruction, he will almost always up his game.

This is exactly what he began to do as I broke out from under some of the lies I had so long believed.

I was rocking along well with my math classes and pre-entry university classes. I had received all A's up to this point. Something began to stir in me as my professors and classmates praised me for my 4.0 GPA. Suddenly, the grades I was getting became an obsession. My goal was no longer to graduate with a nursing degree; it had to be accompanied by a perfect record of the highest achievement. The enemy was setting me up to fail again, and I fell for it hook, line, and sinker.

Again, searching for a new identity, I began creating giants that were not meant for me to fight. Fighting to prove that I was someone because I didn't like the someone who I was. These giants were merely lies that needed more than a sword in my hand to fight; they needed God's healing salve of truth. Yet, I was too busy fighting in my own strength to see.

Sucker Punch

Things started to unravel for me as I took my first English class. After writing my first paper for a homework assignment, I confidently turned it in. It didn't take too long for that confidence to be knocked out of me like someone had punched me straight in the gut – 24 hours, to be exact. As I looked at the C- staring back at me, the lies crept back in. *You are not smart.* Doubting my ability to pull off an "A" in this class with my intellectual capacity, I turned on my feminine charm and resorted to sweet-talking my professor into helping me with my future papers. Thankfully, he genuinely wanted to help me and didn't take everything I would have offered had he taken advantage of it. We worked together daily, one revised paper at a time, to pull off another "A" for the transcript.

Upon completing every quarter, I would hold the transcript of grades and feel the accomplishment I thought it gave me. It had now become an addiction to perfection. I didn't see that one coming, as it slipped right under my nose.

With one more English class to go, I was nervous. The previous one had been a real struggle, and I again doubted myself. We wrote ten papers in 12 weeks. My professor was tough, and she wasn't keen on sweet talk. Believe me, I tried.

After my first paper was returned, it looked like her red pen had exploded all over my writings. Staying behind after class, I explained to her that I needed to make an A in this class. She looked at me and said, "It's okay to make a B. That is a good passing grade. I don't give out A's in my class." *Great.*

Determined to convince her otherwise, I stayed behind after every class asking her how I could rewrite each returned paper to improve my grade. Every time she offered extra credit work, I jumped on it. As the final grade was posted, I prevailed and pulled off an "A" within 1/10 of a point. I laughed to myself, thinking, *she probably wasn't good at math.*

I didn't make it out of nursing school with a 4.0. There would be one B on my transcript. It was in psych nursing, which was one of my favorite classes. On my way to class on a big test day, my car was hit from behind while sitting at a red light. Regardless of the accident, I made it to class and chose to take the remaining time to take my test. As I turned it in, I failed to see the two questions printed on the back side; hence, they were left unanswered. Nursing school was strict regarding foolish mistakes. They trained you to realize that one mistake in the field could mean someone's life. Ironically, I missed my A within 1/10 of a point.

Nursing school was tough. It would be one of the hardest things I have ever accomplished. Despite this reality, I was still disappointed when I graduated with a 3.96 and missed achieving that 4.0 GPA goal. Sounds crazy, huh? I can see that now. However, back then, I was not able to see clearly. My mind was clouded with new lies telling me without perfection, all I had was a failure. It was all or none.

Battle of the Mind

Our minds are a powerful tool. We are the only beings God created with such complexity to choose our thoughts. I was not choosing thoughts that brought about healthy outcomes. Each unhealthy thought would lead to a multitude of more unhealthy thoughts. It was a never-ending cycle of setting myself up with unrealistic perfectionistic goals that I was sure not to meet.

When failure came, it would emotionally manifest into depression. I would stay in this emotional state until the next opportunity to prove myself through performance or status. I was constantly searching for something or someone to prove my worth.

Thank you, Lord, that I have since learned the importance of guarding my mind and taking every thought captive to line it up with Your Word. We cannot simply allow our thoughts to run wild. We must choose thoughts that bring about healthy outcomes and throw out the thoughts that don't serve us.

How do we do this?

Romans 12:2 tells us, "Do not be conformed to this world, but be transformed by the renewal of your mind, that by testing you may discern what is the will of God, what is good and acceptable and perfect."

Philippians 4:8 says, "Finally, brothers and sisters, whatever is true, whatever is noble, whatever is right, whatever is pure, whatever is lovely, whatever is admirable – if anything is excellent or praiseworthy – think about such things."

Your first step is to pay attention to your thought patterns. Are your thoughts life-giving, or do they tear you or others down? The latter is the world's way of thinking. We want to renew our minds to align with what the His Word tells us.

We can only know what the Word tells us by spending time in it and learning its meaning. God will speak to you through His Word. Jeremiah 29:13 says, "You will seek me and find me when you seek me with all your heart."

Going to Him to ask is another great option. When we find ourselves thinking things that contradict Philippians 4:8, we can ask Him what He wants us to know about our thinking. When I hear thoughts that aren't serving my good, I get out my journal and ask, "Lord, what do You want to show me about these thoughts? Where are they coming from? What true, pure, lovely, admirable thought do You want me to replace them with?" As I write down each question, I anticipate His reply. He will answer me as I write down everything that comes to my mind.

God does not want us to fall into the trap of worldly thought patterns. He wants to show us a better way. Start today, if you haven't yet, to incorporate a quiet time every day to read from His Word. Ask Him to show you the negative thoughts, thoughts that are not for you, and speak His truths instead. We must consciously renew our minds daily; it is easiest and most successfully done while spending time in His Word and presence.

As I have begun to be consistent with my morning coffee dates with God (as I call them), I have gained the ability to recognize when my thoughts don't line up with His. Many times, as a negative thought enters my mind, I am immediately reminded of a verse in His Word that combats it. I haven't spent hours a day memorizing scriptures; I have just spent time with Him forming a genuine love relationship. In return, He has written His Word on my heart.

7

Mirror, Mirror

After graduating from nursing school, I accepted a weekend position at a large hospital located 72 miles from my home, moving into a small apartment right across the street. It was nice to be getting away from my troubled marriage. I began working as many extra hours as the hospital would allow. Working 12-hour shifts four to five days a week allowed me to form strong bonds with my new co-workers.

I desperately needed to know that I had not lost my ability to be loved. The enemy knew this was a strong desire, and he wasted no time surrounding me with men who gave me that feeling. They would flatter me with words such as, "You are gorgeous," "I love being around you," and my favorite, "How could your husband let you out of his sight?" I took these words to heart and turned them into words of romance and love.

I ended up having an affair with one of my married co-workers. This affair would last until he accepted another job at another hospital and quickly dismissed our relationship. This false sense of love, better known as lust, had fooled me again. At this point, I fell into my deepest depression yet.

On my days off, I would lay in bed all day. I had no desire to get up and eat; all I could do was cry. I made myself get up and go to work because I knew the alternative would be to return to my marriage. I had come too far now; I was not turning back. Yet, I could not live alone. I needed someone in my life who would love me.

Knowing my body was the key to attracting men, every wrinkle and sag became a constant worry that I would never find someone. With the extra flow of money as a nurse, cosmetic surgery became my answer. My looks would be my next obsession.

Afraid to gain any weight, I would go most days only eating one small meal. Small meant one chicken strip and a handful of fries from the hospital cafeteria. Exercise was at least a twice-a-day occurrence. I would run for miles at a time until my legs would cramp. Continuing to battle depression, the doctor gave me so many medications a pill planner was necessary to keep them in order.

I knew this was not what I wanted for my life, but all the medications kept me numb from having to face any of those feelings. Yet, there was still an inner tug inside of me to change, and it would not go away.

Desperate for some relief, I went back to church in my hometown on the one weekend I had off every month. My husband and I were still together. He wanted to mend our marriage, but I was not interested. We pretended everything was okay in front of our mutual friends.

As we grew further apart, I began to pursue the attention of a friend's husband, who was a part of our church. Within a couple of months, we found ourselves in the middle of an affair. With a heart of stone, I persuaded myself that it was okay since his marriage was not going well either, and I deserved better than I was being given. This time I would leave my 18-year marriage for good.

I thought he was everything I had been searching for my entire life. We had so much in common, talking for hours without running out of things to say. Life was finally taking a turn for me. *This time will be different.*

We married on the beach of St. Thomas, US Virgin Islands. Just like the fairytale wedding that every girl dreams about. Jerry had thought of everything. He looked me in the eye and said, "Your life is about to change." I believed it.

My life did change. We began going back to church. Making plans for our future gave me hope that my life would finally be what I had dreamed it would be. Living my dream, I was the happiest I had ever been.

What Happened to My Happily Ever After?

Happiness…oh yeah, happiness is temporary, right? Yes, it was. Around year four, things started to unravel as the honeymoon wore off. Even though my life had changed, I had not changed. I brought the same baggage with me. I had packed it all up neatly for a while; however, when life settled in and it was time to return to reality, it unpacked itself quickly. It was not pretty. I began to feel alone again. I looked to the man of my dreams to fulfill places in my heart that he could not possibly meet. When he would become frustrated from the pressure of these requests, I would become angry and blame him for my disappointments. It was a vicious cycle. We began to drift apart.

He was pouring hours into his physical therapy clinic. Again, I signed up for as many hours at the hospital as possible. We were doing our own thing. After five years of marriage, I began to fall back into the same old habits. We were fighting more and more anytime we were together at home for any length. I became resentful and continued to blame him for the condition of our marriage. The next thing I knew, I had fallen into another affair.

It was one night of total disappointment. I had failed again, doing the one thing I said I would never do. Feeling the shame and guilt of what I had just done, all I wanted to do was go to bed and never wake up again. How could I be that person again? I had made a promise to myself that person was gone forever. I began to hate myself as much as I thought my husband must have hated me. *I deserve to be alone. I do not deserve a happy marriage.* Certainly, I did not deserve anything but the wrath of God, which I knew was about to fall upon my life.

I did not tell anyone what I had done. I continued to pour myself into my job. My husband and I continued to fight often. I knew it was just a matter of time before he left me.

One night after returning from supper, we had argued all the way home. As soon as we pulled up in the driveway, he exited the vehicle and said he had to get away from me. He got in his truck and drove away. Sitting in my car, I tried to hold it in, but all I could do was cry. Fully expecting him to come home later and tell me to pack my bags and leave, I told myself that this was the night.

A few minutes later, as I saw his headlights coming back up the driveway, I was frantically trying to dry up my eyes to cover up my weakness. I braced myself for the scene that was about to play out. It was all too familiar. As he opened the door to my vehicle, I looked straight ahead with a cold, stern face that matched the heart that was barely beating inside my chest.

However, when he slipped into the passenger seat and closed the door, his words were not at all what I expected to hear. As he looked me in the eyes, he said, "I do not want to live without you. I love you." For a moment, I thought I had misunderstood him. This is not how it happened in real life. I had done wrong, and I did not deserve anyone's love. God was supposed to punish me. That is how it had always happened before.

After a long pause, with him waiting for my reply, a thousand thoughts ran through my mind. One stands out clearly in my memory: *He doesn't really mean that. He doesn't want you to leave because your help in the household makes it easier for him to run his businesses.* Despite my reservations and thoughts of his motives, I was willing to give it a chance. Besides that, performing was always a good option; I could make him love me if I put my mind to it.

I Surrender

Later that night, I felt the tugging feeling again – the one that continued to cry out for change. It was so heavy; it refused to be shaken as in previous encounters. Tears would not stop flowing from my eyes, so I hid in my closet until I could compose myself. As soon as I closed the door, my knees became weak, and I had to kneel on the floor. At this point, the tears began to burn as they rolled down my cheeks. This time, I did not try to hold them in. I let them flow freely as I cried out to God with heavy sobs that shook my entire body. I began begging Him to take away the pain and confessing how tired I was of the cycle I continually found myself in. I wanted to change. I wanted a new life. I wanted to believe that someone could love me for who I was and not for what I could do for them.

As the tears continued to roll down my face, peace came over me. Tears that were once prohibited from showing turned into a warmth of healing. While pouring out my heart to Him, I heard Him say, "Angela, that is Me you are searching for. I have been waiting for this moment for you to cry out to Me for relief from your pain. I have been pursuing you all along. The change you seek can only be found in My love. I love you with never-ending love, and you do not have to perform; you don't have to fight. I love you just the way you are. Follow Me, lay down your sword and allow Me to fight for you. Within My protective embrace, I can give you the new life you have been fighting for all these years. I can make you a new creation."

I could feel my heart of stone begin to melt inside of me. Yet, even as I felt the healing begin while kneeling in that closet, I did not believe 100% what I felt or heard. I chose to surrender that night out of desperation, not love for God. I knew the way I was going was not working. I had tried many times in my own ways and strengths to perform and make things happen for me. The white flag was up, and I was giving Him a chance to help me out of my darkness.

However, it would still be a process that would not happen overnight. It would still take me a few more years to find the love built from a relationship with Him. All the hurt, pain, and wounds formed over the years would take time to process and heal. Having made a promise to give Him a chance, I kept my word. It was pure willpower and obedience that started the journey.

That is one of the many great things about God; He is patient, gentle, and unrelenting. He took me as I was that night. He honored my invitation to "show me what You can do." You do not have to be perfect and get everything taken care of in your life to come to Him. In fact, I have found that when we allow Him into all the pain, the ugly, and the brokenness, it becomes much easier to walk because we are not walking alone. He loves us far more than we can ever fathom. We have never seen a love so deep as the one that He offers.

8

It Was His Love

My love story with Jesus did not start like the fairy tale romances in the childhood books. It began with my obedience to do what I told Him I would do as part of the deal. I would seek Him by returning to church and reading my Bible daily. Also, I agreed to follow all the rules that I knew were in the Bible. That is all I knew to offer at that time. He took it.

As I read my Bible daily, He began to speak to me through the Word. It came alive, and I started seeing His true character shine through. My perception began to change from Him being the dominating controller sitting on the throne, waiting for me to mess up, to the lover who had been pursuing me and offering me His embrace of protection when I did fall short.

Rules I thought I had to follow to be a good Christian began making more sense. I began to see them as protective guidelines that a loving Father put into place for my protection rather than a list of fun hijackers.

He opened my eyes to an entirely different world. I began to seek His presence by spending daily quiet time with Him. I sought Him like I would any other relationship I wanted in my life. Just like any of those relationships, I had to spend time getting to know Him before I could have meaningful interaction.

As I began writing love letters to Him through my journaling, I began to view our relationship in the context of Him being the lover of my soul. He had traveled ahead of me to our destination and prepared a life for me in the happily ever after I had always dreamed of. (Which is precisely what He has done.) I began to fall completely, head over heels in love with Him.

My morning Bible reading began to be something I would look forward to instead of a task I had to check off my "I am doing what I promised to do" list. These morning coffee dates with God would keep me growing as I struggled with other things in my life. While processing the hurts He would have me to walk through, I knew He was there with me, continuing to speak to me through His Word as we walked it all together.

You see, accepting a relationship with Him does not exclude you from the trials and the pain. As we have discussed, we live in a broken world where hurt and pain are inevitable. Yet, we can come out on the other side peacefully because He will see us through. He saw me through a lot of healing, which was sometimes downright painful. Knowing He had me in His embrace and it was for my good that He was walking me through these challenging times made it bearable, for sure.

Romans 8:28: "And we know that God causes all things to work together for good to those who love God, to those who are called according to His purpose."

Thank you, Lord, for working all things for the good within me. Thank you for calling me into a purpose that will bring glory to You and Your Kingdom.

Heart Healing

I had some significant heart healing that had to take place within.

Still experiencing considerable amounts of depression, there were many days when I had to make myself get out of bed to start the day. Regardless of how I felt those mornings, I knew every day held a lesson to be learned, so I pushed through, standing on His promise to carry me through.

The first lesson He walked me through is how to love myself. I would need to lay down the lies my little girl had agreed with so many years ago. False identities that told me I was unimportant would have to be replaced with His truth. I would need to see myself through His eyes to see the truth of who I was created to be. As He walked me through this lesson, He would place people along my path to speak life and love into my life. He highlighted truths to me as we had our morning coffee dates. He would give me dreams at night that spoke truths deep into my heart.

Along the way, I slowly began to see myself as His new creation. I no longer looked for my identity in men, accomplishments, or job titles. Being more confident in my identity, I could open up to those around me and share my heart with them. In turn, my heart began to become softer in the process. I was finally seeing what love could look like for me.

As I grew in my love relationship with Him, He began to bring up the wounds from my past that needed the healing touch of His love. He brought them up one by one. I cannot recall a specific order or timeline of the healing process, but I can tell you that He was gentle and only brought to the surface things I was ready to handle at specific times. Every day was a lesson. Thinking back, I am always in awe of His ways, as I can see His timing is perfect in every situation. Healing would take place in one area that seemed out of place for me at the time, only to make perfect sense when the next healing phase would begin. I would realize how much easier it was to face the current issue having found freedom from the prior hurt.

God used my husband and our marriage to show me what true love within a covenant looked like. I realized that Jerry's patient words came from his heart of love for me; that night sitting in my car opened my heart to let a man in like I had never experienced before. He was patient and forgiving as I walked through the healing process with Jesus.

This love of my dreams began to spill out into my marriage and flourish beyond my wildest dreams. No longer was I seeking validation from my husband or desires that he could not fulfill. I was solely relying on God to meet my needs. This gave my husband the freedom to love me in his own personal way. We fought less. We loved more. Life was looking up.

As a couple, we began to seek God together with more passion than ever. This was the key to our marriage surviving as it did. It was not a product of anything that Jerry or I did on our own. It was a direct result of loving God first. He walked alongside us as we sorted out all the mistakes that had led us to that point of brokenness. God came into our marriage and healed all the broken places. His love flowed through us as we put Him at the center of our lives.

This process did not happen overnight or without some pain and struggle. Still, we pushed through, knowing He was with us, and His plan was for forgiveness and restoration.

We continually encouraged each other daily to seek His love first. Unlike other loves we seek in our lives, it is not a jealous love we must be afraid of. Loving God does not take away from my love for my husband. Instead, it has strengthened our relationship with each other. Falling in love with Him first has allowed us to become best friends and lovers, knowing that God is the foundation of our marriage. I have, in turn, received the best of both worlds. I have two men in my life who love me beyond measure. Never would I have ever imagined feeling this kind of love. His love is like no other.

Forgiveness

Forgiveness started with confessing it to God and asking Him for forgiveness for all the hurts I had caused. As He always does, He graciously forgave all my shortcomings and embraced me in His arms as He spoke words of life into me, "My love covers all your sins. Abide in My love, and you will never want for more." Each step of the healing process would usher in more of His love and plant it deep into my heart.

Next, I would start looking outward. I had hurt many people through the years as I pursued my desire to find my own way. As my heart began to soften, I started to grieve over what I had done to them and how I had hurt them and made them feel. Knowing it would not be entirely up to me to repair the damage done, I began to pray for God to show me how to make things right for the people I had betrayed. As he continued to work within my heart, He brought up those opportunities, in His timing, for me to show my heart to those who I had hurt.

The first opportunity came while I was selling some raffle tickets for a charity. I was invited for a lunch date by a lady who wanted to know more about the charity. She happened to be the wife of the fiancé I had treated so cruelly years ago, and she asked if I would be okay if he joined us for lunch. Hesitantly, I agreed, thinking this could be the day he would let me have it and tell me how horrible I was. As the days got closer, my anxiety heightened. Deep down, I knew this was God's timing, and He would be there beside me whatever transpired. However, my flesh was highly apprehensive that this would be anything but a disaster.

It turns out it went relatively smoothly. He and his wife listened to me with compassion as I told them about the charity close to my heart. In turn, they shared some of their life stories with me. Although I did not get a chance to pour out my heart to him over lunch that day, as soon as I got home, I messaged his wife and asked her permission to message him privately. Stepping into the new person I was becoming, I told her exactly what my intentions were so there would be no questions regarding my motives. She welcomed the interaction.

After sending the heartfelt message, I immediately felt another healing release begin. Knowing I could not control the outcome, I trusted God's hands to finish the work in their hearts that He had started. I was ready for whatever came back. Upon hearing back from him regarding my apology and request for forgiveness, he was very kind. He told me we were very young and didn't hold any of my actions against me. His response gave me the faith and confidence I needed to move forward in asking forgiveness from others as I continued to seek God's timing in doing so.

The next opportunity would be years later. One day, while getting ready for a birthday party for my husband's grandkids, I heard from the Lord by an impression dropped into my mind. In the middle of applying my mascara, the thought came through my mind, "Today, you need to ask forgiveness from Lisa." She was Jerry's ex-wife, the one I had betrayed. With them having children together, this was not the first birthday we had attended. Always keeping my distance at these events, because the air was so thick and uncomfortable, I would usually sit off to the side and try to hide.

My anxiety was already escalated before attending, and now I was a nervous wreck knowing I had no choice but to heed His call for the right timing. This opportunity is what I had been seeking prayer for all these years. Yet, it did not make it easy by any means.

It was a hot summer day. The party was held outdoors for the kids to enjoy playing on a giant waterslide. Lisa had stayed in the house the entire time due to recovering from a recent respiratory illness. Things were winding down, and I still had not executed what He had asked of me. As I polished off the last Cheeto from my lunch plate, I used my orange-stained fingers as an excuse to go inside.

After washing and drying my hands, I sat on the end of the couch where she was sitting. We made small talk for a few minutes before I poured out my heart to her and asked for her forgiveness. I did not want her to feel rushed or pressured to respond right then, and I was honestly afraid of what she would say to me. As a result, I told her that I would be open to a future coffee date to answer all the questions she may have for me regarding the betrayal.

God continued to show me how great His love was for all of us. My past prayers had been that when the time came for me to ask forgiveness from her, she would see my fully renewed and repentant heart through our conversation. As I was praying for restoration for the people I hurt, I could see He was working. She was so gracious in her response to me as she told me how she had been praying for me through the years and had already sought forgiveness in her own heart. Wow. Thank you, Lord, for being a God of restoration, seeking to reconcile the wounds of our hearts.

Later that month, Lisa invited me to lunch. Again, I was nervous, praying that whatever questions she asked me, God would give me the answers I could not give myself. So much of my past I could not remember clearly, and I wanted to provide her with the truth to the best of my knowledge. To my surprise, she did not have any questions for me. All she wanted to do was catch up on our personal lives and enjoy each other's company. Again, I am in awe of God's healing power through His love for us.

Out of the Shadows

Unlike other forgiveness conversations that I had sought out, there was one that remained hidden. It was like a black cloud hanging over my head every time I told my testimony to the girls I ministered to in the prison system.

Although my husband knew our marriage was on the ledge of destruction years ago, I had never confessed to him about my affair, nor had I asked for his forgiveness over it.

Of all the apologies I had given, this one made me the most heart-heavy. So many times, the enemy had convinced me that *it was water under the bridge* and *I did not need to stir up old wounds*. Besides that, God had already forgiven me, and that was all that mattered, right? Wrong! Each time the subject of adultery would come up in church, on a television show, or elsewhere, the guilt would consume me. This hidden unconfessed sin was an open door to drag me back into something I had fought so hard to conquer: guilt, shame, and depression. For this reason, I could not overlook it.

Knowing it was coming, I began to pray that God would again work and prepare Jerry's heart for what I needed to say and that He would show me His timing in doing so.

One night, as we were driving home alone from Jerry's newest therapy clinic, God dropped the impression into my mind, "You need to tell him now." Oh boy. We had already traveled 30 minutes toward the one-hour trek home to pick up the kids, so I knew my time was limited for us to be alone. With the music playing in the car, I continued to see the road signs counting down the miles like a timer waiting to go off. Wrestling with the thought of having to ruin a perfect day out together, I tried to convince myself that I had not heard the Lord correctly. However, I had grown to know His voice well and could not deny that He had spoken.

Reaching over to turn off the radio, I told him I needed to talk to him about something important. Immediately I began to cry as I felt the fear well up inside me. Honestly, I don't remember everything I said, but as I was trying to tell him that I had done something I wasn't proud of back when we were falling apart, he said to me, "You are not the person you used to be, and that is all in the past. I forgive you. I love you." He would not let me finish.

As I type this out just now, those healing tears of mercy still flow from my eyes. God continues to use my husband and our marriage daily to show me the power of His love in a way that I can tangibly see.

For years I thought God could not give me what I needed because I could not see or touch Him. I needed things I could put my hands on and see with my eyes to know that I was loved, seen, and heard. Above all, He knows what we need, and He will deliver that to us in the most perfect of ways.

Thank you, Lord, for my husband and my marriage. Thank you for knowing exactly what we need and how to deliver those gifts to us.

9

Every Perfect Gift

Still living in the same small, Southern town, I would often be reminded of my mistakes. I would pass someone on the street who would look the other way to avoid eye contact. Specific landmarks would remind me of situations, and scenes would play out in my mind as if they had just happened yesterday. I could not get away from the memories.

For a while, there was a feeling I could not shake. *All this forgiveness stuff is just too easy. There has to be a catch at some point when I will be punished for my past.* Worrying that I couldn't let my guard down and wondering if God was holding something back to throw in my face later kept me from unlocking total freedom.

I was so afraid to put my trust in anyone…even God. Trust had never served me well in my past. If I let my guard down, I risked being hurt. So, keeping my heart closed off and protecting it at all costs was easier.

Thank goodness He does not allow us to stay in those places. He slowly and patiently walked me through another journey to show His heart toward me. It would be another hard lesson to walk through, yet worth the struggle. This time He would use a house to teach me that I can trust Him with my heart and He is a good Father who does not back down on His promises. James 1:17 tells us, "Every good thing given and every perfect gift is from above, coming down from the Father of lights, with whom there is no variation or shifting shadow." He does not change His mind; He is for us and not against us. His love never fails.

Remember in chapter three when I told you that trust would be the last door to be opened to allow God's healing light in? Well, this is the story that opened the door...

Welcome Home

The home Jerry and I had was the home that he and his previous wife had lived in together. Jerry had wanted to sell the house, but I kept convincing him that we were fine living there. I had made it our own for years, and I was settled. I was fine living there, but he was not. Being ready to leave the past behind and have a fresh start, this house was a constant reminder to him of our past.

To me, this house was the best I had ever lived in as an adult. In my previous marriage, we had lived in a home that needed constant repair. For example, there was a hole in front of the toilet due to weak flooring. Each time you sat on the toilet it was like playing Russian roulette, betting whether or not you would fall through.

This new home was like Cinderella's castle to me. It was a four-bedroom brick home with a fenced-in backyard, in a nice neighborhood, and at the end of the cul-de-sac. I had worked on the yard to get it just like I wanted it – with flowing water fountains, flower beds, and chickens in the backyard. It was my haven.

When Jerry would talk about putting our home on the market, I would get extremely anxious. I was not thinking about his needs. I was too entangled in my issues of mistrust and could not dream of something better.

Honestly, I did not think that God would give me anything better.

Seeing what I had done in my past, I did not deserve anything close to this home. Surely if this house were taken, He would give me exactly what I deserved. I was better off staying where I was. Here I knew what I had, and it was good. Convincing myself that I had to fight to keep what was good for me is precisely what I did.

Tickets Please

It was like standing in line after purchasing your ticket to the roller coaster. Some wait in line with excitement and expectation of the thrill ahead, while others wait with anxiety and fear of what will transpire. Most of the latter group only agreed to the ride because their peers, who fell into the former group, convinced them to do so. I had always hated roller coasters, and this one was no different. I waited for my turn in line to climb into the emotion express.

Jerry and I would attend every open house in our town. He had always loved looking at homes and would get so excited about the tours. Excitement was not on my list of emotions while attending these events. I felt threatened that my world would be uprooted from the safety I thought had been obtained through my new life.

Meanwhile, in his heart, Jerry dreamed of the day we would buy a home to call our own. With each home we looked at, he made a mental list of the things our new home would contain. Again, all I could do was compare everything to our current home, and nothing compared. I was convinced God wanted us to stay right where we were.

So, when my husband came home one day and said it was time to move forward, I was bitter. I prayed daily God would show him what I felt He had already shown me. We were not selling; we were not moving, and we'd be staying right where we were.

Reluctantly, I agreed to put the house up for sale. Being thoroughly convinced we were meant to stay there, I was not surprised when the house had not sold after being on the market for a year. Nevertheless, this year was a roller coaster of emotions while many people would come and go through my home to determine if they liked it enough to put in an offer. I was wholeheartedly trying to be obedient to God and learning to trust Him, but my flesh was fighting to keep what I thought was best for me. Our contract with the real estate agent ended, and Jerry was discouraged that we had not received any offers. Feeling defeated, he became convinced it was God's will for us to stay.

With paper, pencil, and ruler in hand, Jerry began to draw out a plan for us to remodel our current home and together make it into our dream. With that matter settled, I was finally at peace. Looking back on some of my love letters to God during this season, I thanked Him for the peace and for the answer to my prayers of Jerry seeing we needed to stay. I was beginning to have some joy in my life. I was hearing God. He was answering my prayers, I had my dream home, my husband agreed, and we were closing that chapter of life. Next.

If only it were always that simple. Isaiah 55:8 tells us, "'For My thoughts are not your thoughts, nor are your ways My ways,' declares the Lord."

During church service only two weeks later, Jerry received a text from our agent stating there was a young couple who had looked at our home while it was still on the market and wanted to look one more time. I froze in terror as I reminded Jerry we had already agreed we were no longer selling. "Tell them NO!"

His words to me were, "It won't hurt to let them look." So, we did. That day we rushed home to clean up the house for them to look that afternoon. As I was putting away dishes, the bitterness came rolling back in. "Lord, when will this end? I am tired. I need closure. I need peace. I need joy."

After looking at our house, we immediately received a text from the young couple's agent with an offer within the hour. They offered exactly what we were asking. Feeling defeated and confused, I gave in, and we accepted the offer. Still trying to be obedient to God and trust Him, I reluctantly went to look at new houses the next day, and then again the next day. Every time it was the same old story; nothing compared to what I had. We looked at one more house as I was about to give up and throw in the towel. For the first time in this house-hunting journey, I could see a vision of better things to come. It was a beautiful home, and I fell in love with it immediately. We both agreed this would be our forever home and new beginning.

We put in an offer on our new dream home and began planning how we would set it up. Visiting the furniture store, we picked out a new sofa sectional that would look amazing. We had the best time searching antique stores for light fixtures and fun décor. Again, I had peace. Things started to look brighter again. *I am sorry, Lord, that I did not trust You. Thank you for this opportunity to grow as I let go and allow You to work.*

Again, some lessons are harder to learn, and our faith will be tested. Ten days later, the breath would be knocked out of me again. The young couple had visited the bank and felt they could not afford the payments for a new home. They backed out. We, in turn, had to back out of our contract on the house I now had my heart set on.

I received the phone call while driving home one day. As the words rang in my ear, I had to pull over on the side of the road. My heart and my mind were a total mess. My emotions overcame me as I belted out a scream that sounded like a wild banshee. I yelled to God, "What the hell do you want from me?" Yes, I cussed at God in anger, hurt, disappointment, fear, and confusion. I tell you, my friend, it was not a pretty scene. All the emotion just rushed through me at once. I felt out of control. I WAS out of control. Thank the Lord no one was around to see me, as I was scaring myself.

Yet God was not afraid of my emotion. Although I later asked for forgiveness for my disrespect toward Him at that moment, He lovingly forgave and allowed me to process all the feelings pulsing through my veins. I did not understand what was happening. I continued to ask, "God, what are You trying to teach me in all of this? What am I missing? Just show me because I do not know how much more I can take."

I wanted to believe that He had my good in mind, yet I knew I deserved so much less. Being in a constant state of confusion, I questioned the things happening. *Are You going to punish me or not? Is this the punishment You are dealing out? Will I live in a constant state of limbo? Everyone keeps telling me You have my best in mind. Why does it hurt so much?*

Silence was all I heard.

I did not get my answer right away. It would take more time for this question to be addressed. That is a complex concept for most of us...the waiting. Waiting is tough when things do not seem to be moving in the right direction after you have done everything you thought was right. If you are in that place now, have hope. He works even when you cannot see, hear, or feel it. Trust that He has your best in mind even when things seem to be falling apart.

My loving husband felt so heavy. He was disappointed for himself because he could not move forward in his dream of a fresh start, and he was sad my life had again been turned upside down after finding peace in our decision to move.

He assured me we could go back to our original plan he already had drawn up for renovating the home and making it our own. I wish I could say I processed all this with grace and trusted that God would work it out for my good. Nope, I had not learned that lesson yet. At this point, I did not even care about any of it. The mention of houses made me want to throw up. Deciding to let Jerry make the decisions on all of it, I was done! Checking out and being numb was one of my defense mechanisms to keep me safe.

On the other hand, when the numbness would wear off, the lack of control would make me crazy. Feeling too vulnerable, handing over control did not last very long. I decided we should put the house on the market and keep it there until it sold, or we died, whichever came first. Can you hear the stubbornness coming through? I was determined to control this situation one way or another. Yet, taking back control did not make me happy either. What little joy I had obtained was now gone again. Nothing satisfied me.

Regardless, I would continue to seek God and grow in my relationship with Him. Reading from His Word, writing my love letters, and having our dates together kept my heart pliable, although part of my heart was still closed off to anyone, including Him. I am so thankful that He is such a gentleman and does not push us away during these times. He is ultimately after our hearts and will wait patiently while we sort through our mess and decide to give everything over to Him in complete surrender. Little did I know that was the very lesson He was teaching me through this battle.

It was a daily struggle of constant roller-coaster emotions. In hindsight, I can see the problem was me not surrendering this situation to Him, and I was carrying it on my own. I would pray for Him to help me through it, yet I refused to let go. I was afraid of being hurt again by relinquishing my control and trusting Him with my whole heart.

Can I please exchange my coaster ticket for something safer, like the carousel?

It Is Well

During this time, I began to serve with a group of women who ministered in the prison system and started teaching a Bible study to the women housed there. One of the women on the team became a close spiritual mentor for me; I shared my story and struggles with the house situation with her.

She encouraged me to list all the things I wanted in a dream home – to write them down and not leave out any details. Although I admired her, I was not interested in making any list. I did not care what the house looked like; I was just ready to be settled. She continued to encourage (nag) me until I did it.

I remember sitting down with my stubborn attitude, reluctantly writing the list. I wrote down everything I could remember liking in the hundreds of homes we had looked at over the past three years. I even wrote down what my husband wanted in a home, all while continuing to think this was a waste of my time. *There is no way one house could have all of this unless we built it ourselves.* My list included a soaking tub with a crystal chandelier hanging above it, a large shower with rain shower head, a sunroom with large windows to have lots of plants, a large backyard for my chickens and animals, a separate porch to overlook the backyard and have a bed swing, a large kitchen island, a walk-in pantry, a large laundry room, front porch with room for rocking chairs, flower beds with no bushes, and the house itself must be in a cul-de-sac. These were just a few items on my long impossible list.

I finished the list, told my friend I did it, packed it away, and forgot about it.

As I continued to seek God and listen to my spiritual mentor friend, I began to hand it over to Him a little bit at a time, eventually reaching a point where I laid it all at His feet and left it there. It was not an easy process. Lots of tears, prayers, and more tears transpired through that process. Yet, He had not let me down on anything else thus far, so I gave it a chance. When I did, I received such peace. For the first time in my life, I could honestly say to Him, "Whatever You have for me, Lord, I will be content with."

After seven more months, our house finally sold, and it was time to find our new home. Our dream home we had an offer on the previous year was still on the market. We had kept our eye on it and knew it was destined to be ours. We immediately put in another bid on it and waited for our return call. We received the call, but it was not the one we expected. It seemed like one of those movie scenes when everything goes into slow motion. The agent informed us that an offer had been accepted only minutes before our offer came through. *What? Is this happening, Lord?*

Again, I was deflated. Not angry or numb this time, just extremely disappointed. I thought I had it figured out this time. Silly girl. Yet, through it all, I had peace that God was in control now. It had shifted from a fear of not being in power to a peace that I did not have to be. The couple buying our home was not going to move in for another four months, so we had time to look for a house. We had been looking all along, but there was nothing that caught our eye. I was tired of looking and told Jerry to decide. Again, this time it was not me checking out and becoming numb; it was a complete peace that Jerry would be able to pick out what we needed. I prayed for God to open doors to the home that He wanted for us, and I was at peace even though none of the houses compared to what I was leaving behind or the home I had wanted.

Jerry found a house that we both agreed on. It needed some

remodeling to make it our own, but it was going up for auction at a reasonable price. We both agreed that this was the one God had led us to. Again, I was not excited about it. Nevertheless, I had peace.

But God

The auction would take place on Saturday morning, and we were prepared to walk away with our forever home. As I was in town running errands on Friday evening before the big day, a text came across my phone from a friend at church. She had been looking on Facebook and saw someone had posted a house for sale by the owner and thought about me. Looking at the pictures, I thought it was a beautiful home, but there was no need to look because we had decided already. My wild ride was about to come to an end where I would get to settle down and be content.

Knowing my friend would ask on Sunday morning if we looked at the house, I mentioned it to Jerry and showed him the pictures when he got home. I was not surprised when he suggested we look at the house, thinking we could get some remodeling ideas from it.

Honestly, I did not want to look at another house, especially since we had already closed the house hunting chapter, and I was about to have my limbo state over. However, I called the number listed and apologized for calling so late, telling the owner I would understand if she did not want to show us the house because it was getting dark already. To my surprise, she said come on over.

As we drove up to the house, which sat in a cul-de-sac, my eyes lit up! It was beautiful from the outside. The flower beds were full of old-fashioned plants and flowers with no bushes to be seen. There were even some irises in the front flower bed. As we entered the house, I fell in love at every turn. On the inside, I felt so overwhelmed with my emotions.

On the one hand, I was dreaming of what it would be like to call this home. On the other hand, I was so tired of the process and kept reminding myself a decision had already been made. It was finished. At several points, I teared up, but I forced myself not to think about it because I knew my husband wanted a bigger house. (This one was only three bedrooms.) As we pulled out of the driveway after our tour, he asked me, "Well, what did you think of the house?"

"I loved it.," I replied blankly. Something began to stir in me again as he smiled and said, "Me too! Let's make an offer."

The rest is history. We made our offer that night, signed the paperwork the following day, and moved in two weeks later.

Letting It Sink In

During the first few days of unpacking, I found the list I had reluctantly made at my friend's prompting. I knew this house held most of the things I wanted, but I was wrecked as I reviewed the list. Every single item on the list was in this house, and many other wonderful things I had not thought of.

When I tell you everything, yes! Even the exact pebble stone tile in the shower we had previously picked out for the other home was there! The owner told us this tile was not the one she had ordered to be installed but kept it anyway since they had already finished the job while she was at work. *Are you kidding me? No, they installed the correct tile that was supposed to be there!* All I could do was cry tears of joy, awe, and overwhelming gratitude. This entire time, I had thought I would have to settle for less because I did not deserve any better. Yet, here was my God of mercy and grace, giving me more than I had even dreamed for.

Every time I drive up to my home and walk in the door, every time I sit at our dining room table or lay in my bed at night, I am reminded of the gift He gave to me. It is a tangible reminder of how much He loves me, and no matter what I have done in my past, I can trust Him not to hold it over my head. I am loved, I am wanted, I am seen, I am heard, and most importantly, I am forgiven and redeemed.

I am also reminded of how hard I fought against Him to keep what I thought was best for me in the old home. He knows our wants and needs so much more than we do. If we allow Him to work for our good and lay all our own plans down, He will never fail us.

Even though I love my home, it is not about the physical dwelling. I can honestly say if I lost it tomorrow, my faith would carry me through, trusting He has me in His hands. It is about the details. When I look around, I see His heart in all the details. Although years have passed since the day we moved in, I still sit and cry tears of gratitude and joy that He loved me enough to put so much thought into the details of what would make me smile. He cares about the details, my friend. Nothing is too small for Him when it comes to His precious daughters.

If you'd like to watch a video about our miracle house,
*visit **LoveRedeemedMe.com** today.*

10

Happily Ever After

The question I get asked to talk about most often is, "How do I find that love relationship with Jesus like you have?" As I have tried to put some framework in place as a guide for women to follow, I have found there is not a precise blueprint for this process. That may seem like bad news if you, like me, prefer a black and white answer and a checklist approach. Yet, take heart; it is so much better than that. It is a personal process, playing out as a daily adventure with Him. Every love story will look different. We all have different personalities and unique gifts and desires that He has placed inside us.

It looks a little different for everyone because He meets you personally to speak His love in your language. As you accept this adventure, He will take you to places you never dreamed of. Like me, you will look back one day and wonder who you have become and how the heck you got there!

Building a relationship with anyone, including God, is a process. Just like our human relationships, there is no cookie-cutter formula in building each of them. Relationships are built by spending time together and getting to know each other. Similarly, our relationship will be grown with God as we spend quality time getting to know Him through His Word, quiet time daily, and continuous prayer.

Funny, as I wrote the last sentence, I was taken back to a time in my life when I would do those things and wonder why it was not working for me. So let me expound on those relationship building blocks.

First, let us look at quality time in a human-to-human relationship. Do you spend time with your best friend, always talking about yourself and never seeking to learn what they like or who they are inside? Do you ask a question and never listen for their answers? Are you always asking your friend to handle the problems in your life, and that is the only time you converse? Hopefully not! If so, I would be willing to bet the relationship will not last long.

A solid friendship is composed of two people sharing life. It consists of back-and-forth conversations about things you both have in common and enjoy. You talk, but you also listen. It is built on trust developed over time – trusting your friend has your best in mind. You enjoy spending time with them and care about what they care about. When they hurt, you hurt. When they are full of joy, you celebrate with them.

Our relationship with God should look just like this example. When I say we should get to know Him through His Word, I do not mean reading the Word so we can check it off our daily list. That takes us directly back to the performance mindset. We should read in expectation of getting to know who He was and still is.

Our quiet time daily should not be a timer set to accomplish a task. In contrast, it should be time when we welcome and enjoy His presence as we thank Him for what He brings into our lives, and we keep our heart open to listen to what He wants to say.

Continuous prayer does not look like kneeling beside your bed with your hands folded, eyes closed, and uttering fancy words that feel religious. Prayer is a conversation with God. As we go through our day, we can have a continuous dialogue.

As human beings, we have made it so complicated to follow and love Him. We have made up all these rules and regulations that must be followed in order to come to Him and be loved by Him. Checklists, religious rituals, striving, fighting, performing, and earning His love are not part of the plan.

He wants our hearts. It is that simple.

Before you start to hear what I am *not* saying, let me interject. We cannot be living like wild hooligans by night and His children by day. However, you do not have to have it sorted out to begin a relationship with Him. As His love begins to penetrate the depths of your heart – and it will – you will start to see life through a new lens. You will begin to see what true love looks like through the eyes of a loving Father. In return, your desires will align with His purpose for your life. At that moment, you will begin to experience healing and freedom, which will lead to the most amazing life adventure.

Making Love Last

The other question I get asked most often is, "How do you stay in love?"

That question is answered in the same way as the first. How do we stay in love in a human relationship? We continue to pursue each other, have regular dates, and remember and be thankful for the reason we fell in love in the first place.

Continuing to pursue Him means staying in the Word and continuing to grow in wisdom. This pursuant relationship is something you must never neglect. Every time I read from the Bible, I discover something new about God that is just what I need to hear for that day.

In addition to my regular quiet times with God, I regularly plan a date with Him. These dates may look like listening to praise and worship music as I walk through my neighborhood, or it may look like having a picnic by the lake as I journal all the ways He brings joy to my life. Being creative with your dates with God will help you look for Him in places you would not usually think to find Him.

I start and end my days by thanking Him and praising Him for the blessings He brings into my life. No matter what is going on in life, you can always find some things to be thankful for. Thankfulness is also a game-changer. Thankfulness and negativity cannot dwell together. Starting the day off with thankfulness and praise is a great way to set the tone for the rest of your day.

Finding things to be thankful for during the first couple of years was critical for my mental health. Many days were dark, and I was still fighting to make myself get out of bed and live out my day.

I started by journaling my thoughts of thankfulness. Today, I love to look back and see how far I have come from where I used to be. Those journal entries would later turn into my love letters to God, where I would express my love and tell Him the secrets of my heart.

To this day, I continue to write love letters to Him. I always start with thanking Him for at least three things in my life. Of those three things, I make it a point for two of them to refer to Him personally and ways I am thankful for what He brings into my life.

Here is a recent example of the beginning of one of my love letters: "Good morning, Lord! Thank you for the good night's rest I had last night. Thank you for the soft covers that kept me warm and dry through the night. Thank you for the fresh, hot coffee and our morning date we are sharing. I love You, Lord. Thank you for the peace You bring into my life. Thank you for turning my mourning into joy. Lord, You have my whole heart. You are my everything. You get my first breath in the morning and my dreams at night. Again, I love You, Lord. I cannot wait to see what adventure You have planned for us today."

If you apply these tools I have suggested, I know He will meet you where you are, and you will find a love story of your own. I finally found my purpose. You will too. I found the deepest love relationship with my Jesus. You will too. Within that love story, I can be exactly who He has created me to be. You will too. I not only fell deeply in love with Him, but I was also able to fall in love myself. You will too.

This Is Not the End

I pray that my story has given you hope to pursue a new love relationship with Him or grow deeper in your existing relationship.

Before closing this chapter of our journey together, I want to encourage you to find a group of friends who share your dreams and desires, and get plugged into those relationships. As I was going through some of those dark times, He sent people into my life to encourage me, pray for me, and push me forward when I did not feel like I could continue on my own. I will be forever grateful for those friends in my life.

God never intended for us to live alone. He made us to enjoy each others' companionship. If you are missing those relationships in your life now, or if you want more of those godly relationships, I would love to invite you into my community of friends sharing life. You can find my social media links, upcoming events, and sign up for my email list today by visiting LoveRedeemedMe.com. I cannot wait to get to know you more and hear what God is doing in your life.

Love you so much, my friend.

Author's Note

Leave it to God to throw a surprise in after everything has been written. As I was sitting on my back porch bed swing one day, thinking about this first book journey, a memory from long ago dropped into my head. I had completely forgotten this memory.

Do you remember what that is called? That is correct: an *impression.*

I was in sixth grade. My teacher that year had our class write a story for creative writing. Mine was titled, "The Life of a Piece of Bubble Gum." The main character was, you guessed it, a stick of bubble gum. He was lying on the store shelf, when a little girl purchased him, chewed him up, and spit him out on the sidewalk. The story was built around the journey of this bubble gum as he got stuck on the bottom of someone's shoe, then to a car tire, and finally was plucked from the ground and taken on an adventure by a curious bird.

As I thought about the memory, I remember thoroughly enjoying the writing of that story as a little girl.

To my surprise, at the end of the school year, on awards day, the teacher called my name to receive a writing award. She had sent my story into a contest, and I had won! I was so surprised and full of excitement over that achievement.

How could I have forgotten about that as I struggled with writing again many years later? It is just another example of how deep those lies can reach into your heart and mind and convince you of perceived limitations in your life.

Now, I can see how I've always had it in me to be a writer. I can't wait to get started on the next one!

So, what has always been in your heart to do? Give those dreams to God and see them soar!

Thank You

This journey was not one I could have accomplished on my own.

First and foremost, thank you, Lord, for not giving up on me as I wrestled with this assignment. You are the most amazing God. I have grown beyond my wildest dreams as we have written my story together. Thank you for loving me with a love like no other. I love You.

My wonderful husband, Jerry, for always believing in me. You have been a true picture of the Ephesians 5:25 husband. I could not have asked for anyone better. I love you.

My best girlfriend, Tara, for being patient while I had to skip many of our girl dates to write. Thank you for always encouraging me with words of wisdom and praying with me when I called to say, "I don't think I can do this!"

Mrs. Elizabeth Foy, for encouraging me to lay down perfection and chose obedience. You have been a great encourager on this journey. So happy our paths crossed again.

Sandi, for the many pep talks and author moments shared together as you encouraged me to press onward.

Krista, my wonderful editor, for taking my words and perfecting them before they were sent out into the world. You have been the most wonderful friend through this process. Thank you for using your gifts to help others get their stories out.

All my 100X family, there are way too many to list here. (That would take another entire book.) I am so incredibly blessed to have such a community of friends who support each other in business as we do. Thank you for loving me.

My book launch team, thank you for being the first readers of my final draft. You all hold a special place in my heart, and thank you for taking the time to give your feedback and help me get the word out. I look forward to many more book launches with you. I love you, y'all.

About the Author

Angela Yarborough has a passion to see women set free from the lies of their pasts and begin living in the love and freedom of Christ. Having accomplished this in her own life, she regularly speaks to women and gives them hope for a love story of their own.

Combining her business knowledge, creative gifting, and love for the women she is called to serve, Angela has built an online jewelry business that employs women coming from the prison system or sex trade industry. AmadeaDesigns.com equips women with the skills they need to obtain a long-term job that fits their God-given talents.

Living in a small town in North Louisiana with her husband, Jerry, along with their last two kids at home, daily adventures in nature bring a smile to her face. Picnics by the lake, kayaking on the river, and playing with her pet goats and sassy chickens are just a few things you might find Angela doing when she is not designing jewelry, writing books, or ministering to women.

To learn more about Angela and her adventures, book her for a speaking engagement, or to download the companion questions to this book visit: **LoveRedeemedMe.com**.

@angela.l.yarborough

@angela.l.yarborough

JEWELRY WITH HEART

The word Amadea means *God's beloved*.

Amadea is a company that was born out of a passion to empower women with the tools they need to start a new and abundant life after leaving the sex trade industry and/or prison system. Founder, Angela Yarborough, saw a need for these women, since they were not easily employed in the workplace. Most lacked skills to obtain and hold a fulfilling job.

Our mission at Amadea is to provide a loving and supportive work environment for these women as they learn and grow in their job skills and work ethics. We help them build a solid resume that will allow them to transition to a job that fits their God-given gifts and purpose.

By supporting our company, you are providing a job for these women that will have a lasting impact on their future. While growing in their work ethics, they are also developing a sense of who God created them to be.

These women are truly transformed as they develop confidence in their abilities to co-create with God and begin a different story.

Visit our online store at

https://AmadeaDesigns.com

and make a difference in the lives of women!

If this book stirred something in your heart and you'd like to go deeper into this topic, watch videos, and access some discussion questions, join me now at:

LoveRedeemedMe.com

If you enjoyed this book, please consider leaving a positive review on Amazon and Goodreads!

Published with help from

Made in the USA
Columbia, SC
11 June 2024

36982223R00065